B L U E P R I N T
History Key Stage
Copymasters

Second Edition

Joy Palmer

Stanley Thornes (Publishers) Ltd

Do you receive *BLUEPRINTS NEWS*?

Blueprints is an expanding series of practical teacher's ideas books and photocopiable resources for use in primary schools. Books are available for separate infant and junior age ranges for every core and foundation subject, as well as for an ever widening range of other primary teaching needs. These include **Blueprints Primary English** books and **Blueprints Resource Banks**. **Blueprints** are carefully structured around the demands of the National Curriculum in England and Wales, but are used successfully by schools and teachers in Scotland, Northern Ireland and elsewhere.

Blueprints provide:
- *Total curriculum coverage*
- *Hundreds of practical ideas*
- *Books specifically for the age range you teach*
- *Flexible resources for the whole school or for individual teachers*
- *Excellent photocopiable sheets – ideal for assessment and children's work profiles*
- *Supreme value.*

Books may be bought by credit card over the telephone and information obtained on **(01242) 577944**. Alternatively, photocopy and return this **FREEPOST** form to receive **Blueprints News**, our regular update on all new and existing titles. You may also like to add the name of a friend who would be interested in being on the mailing list.

Please add my name to the **BLUEPRINTS NEWS** mailing list.

Mr/Mrs/Miss/Ms _____

Home address _____

_____ Postcode _____

School address _____

_____ Postcode _____

Please also send **BLUEPRINTS NEWS** to:

Mr/Mrs/Miss/Ms _____

Address _____

_____ Postcode _____

To: Marketing Services Dept., Stanley Thornes Ltd, FREEPOST (GR 782), Cheltenham, GL50 1BR

First published in 1992
2nd edition 1996

First published in new binding in 1998 by
Stanley Thornes (Publishers) Ltd
Ellenborough House
Wellington Street
CHELTENHAM GL50 1YW

98 99 00 01 02 / 10 9 8 7 6 5 4 3 2 1

A catalogue record for this book is available from the British Library.

ISBN 0–7487–3427–9

Typeset by Tech-Set, Gateshead, Tyne & Wear.
Printed and bound in Great Britain by
Redwood Books, Trowbridge, Wiltshire

CONTENTS

INTRODUCTION

In this book there are 105 photocopiable copymasters linked to many of the activities in the Teacher's Resource Book. Where the copymasters are referred to in the text of the Teacher's Resource Book there are instructions on how to use them. They are referred to by numbers in the Teacher's Resource Book by this symbol 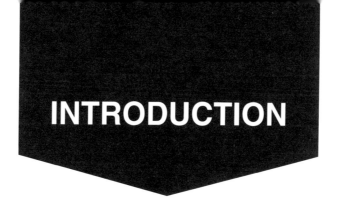 . The copymasters reinforce and extend activities in the Teacher's Resource Book and provide opportunities to record activities and results in an organised way. When the children have completed these copymasters they can be added to work files or used as exemplar material in pupil profiles. You may also wish to use completed copymasters as a resource for your assessments. There is one record sheet at the back of the book (copymaster 106) on which you can make your comments on the children's experience of the National Curriculum.

The copymasters are organised according to the National Curriculum Study Units which are covered in depth in the Teacher's Resource Book. Sheets 91–105 develop general historical skills for Key Stage 2. You will find an explanation of how to use them at the front of the Teacher's Resource Book.

Name: _____

The growth of the Roman Empire

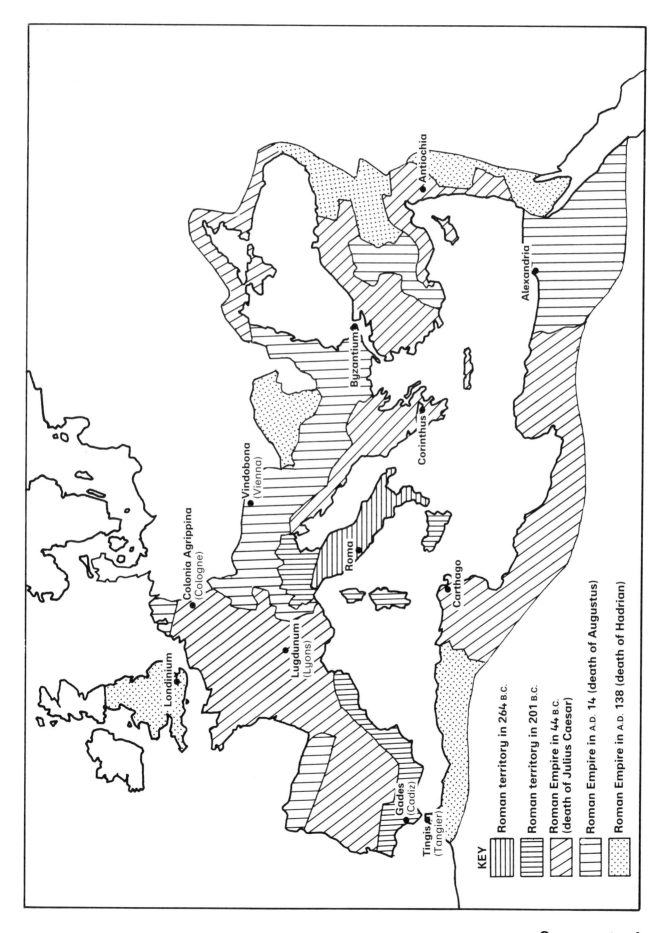

KEY

- Roman territory in 264 B.C.
- Roman territory in 201 B.C.
- Roman Empire in 44 B.C. (death of Julius Caesar)
- Roman Empire in A.D. 14 (death of Augustus)
- Roman Empire in A.D. 138 (death of Hadrian)

Cities labelled on map: Antiochia, Alexandria, Byzantium, Corinthus, Vindobona (Vienna), Colonia Agrippina (Cologne), Roma, Carthago, Lugdunum (Lyons), Londinium, Gades (Cadiz), Tingis (Tangier)

Name: _____

Claudius invades Britain

A Roman legionary

Be a Roman reporter

The ROMAN TIMES

A.D. 43   Vol. IV No. XIII

In praise of the Emperor Claudius

Roads and forts

Scale 0   **50 miles**

▉▉ **Legionary fortress**

■ **Fort**
(not all forts are shown)

═══ **Road**

Mouth of R. Forth

Antonine Wall

Mouth of R. Clyde

PICTS

Solway Firth

Hadrian's Wall

Mouth of R. Tyne

Irish Sea

North Sea

The Wash

Branchester

Burgh Castle

Fosse Way

Ermine Street

Watling Street

WELSH

Gloucester

Colchester

Walton Castle

Bradwell

Caerleon

Reculver

Richborough

Dover

Chichester

Lympne

Porchester

Pevensey

Carisbrooke

English Channel

SAXON — — — SHORE

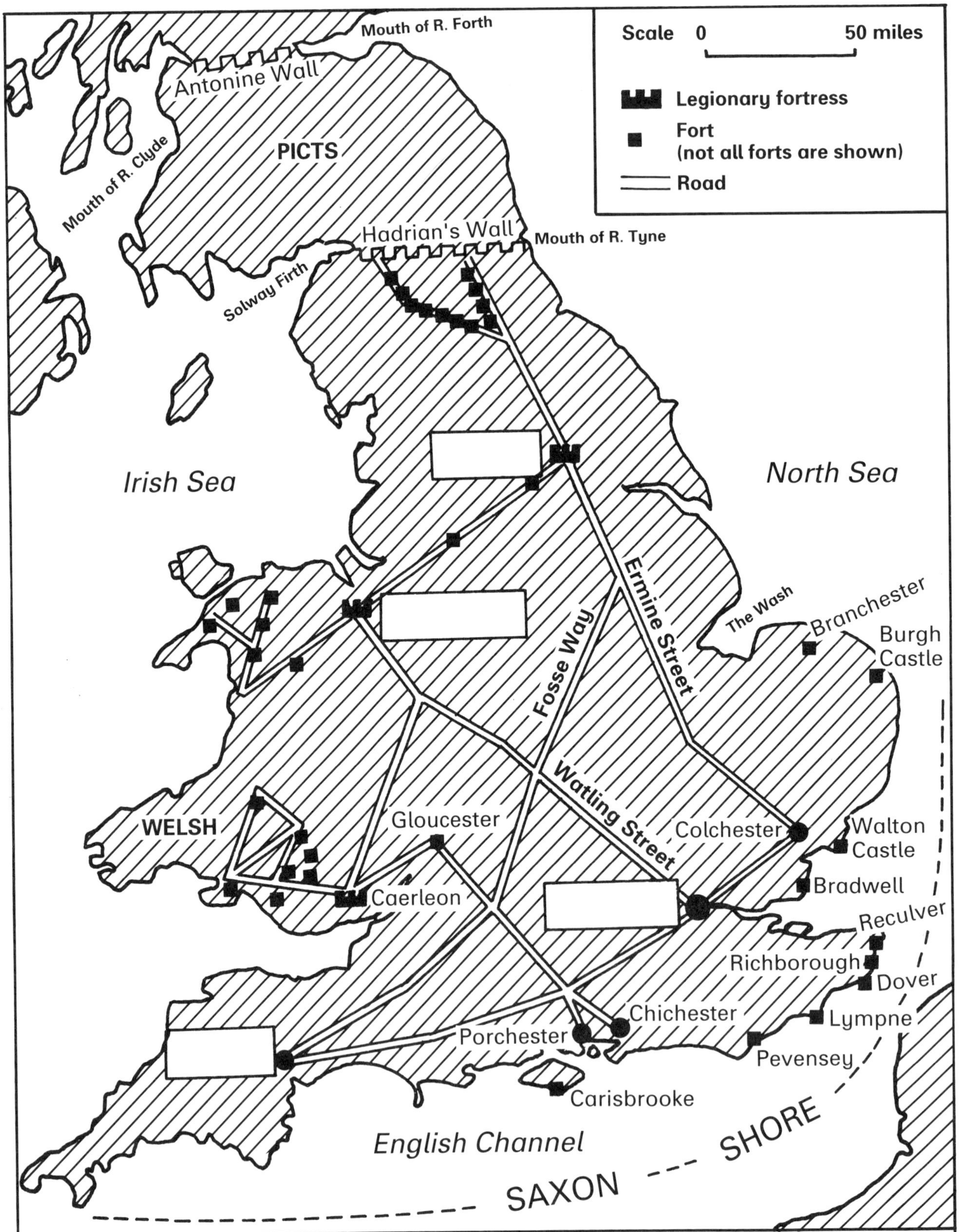

Sort out these place-names
and put them in the boxes
on the map.

KRYO	NOLNDO
EHSTCRE	TEERXE

Copymaster 4

Name: _____

A Roman villa

In the kitchen

The atrium

A Roman bath

Plan of a Roman villa

NYMPHEUM

FURNACE

TANK

TANK

BASIN

TANK

COLONNADE

BATHS

HOT BATH

BED

BED

E. PORTICUS

ENTRANCE

W. PORTICUS

TRICLINIUM

LODGE

Name: _____

A dinner party

MENU

Roman numerals

I	II	III	IV	V	VI	VII	VIII	IX	X
1	2	3	4	5	6	7	8	9	10

XI	XII	XIII	XIV	XV		
11	12	13	14	15	16	17

		XX
18	19	20

L	C	D	M
50	100	500	1000

X + V = ☐

II + XI +V = ☐

XX – XIV = ☐

XI + IV – I = ☐

X × V = ☐

D ÷ C = ☐

C – L – XX – X = ☐

XVI ÷ IV = ☐

Gods and goddesses

Neptune, god of the _____

Venus, goddess of _____

Mars, god of _____

Jupiter, god of _____

Ceres, goddess of _____

Name: _____

The legacy of settlement

LEGACY OF ROME

Name: _____

The Anglo-Saxon invasion

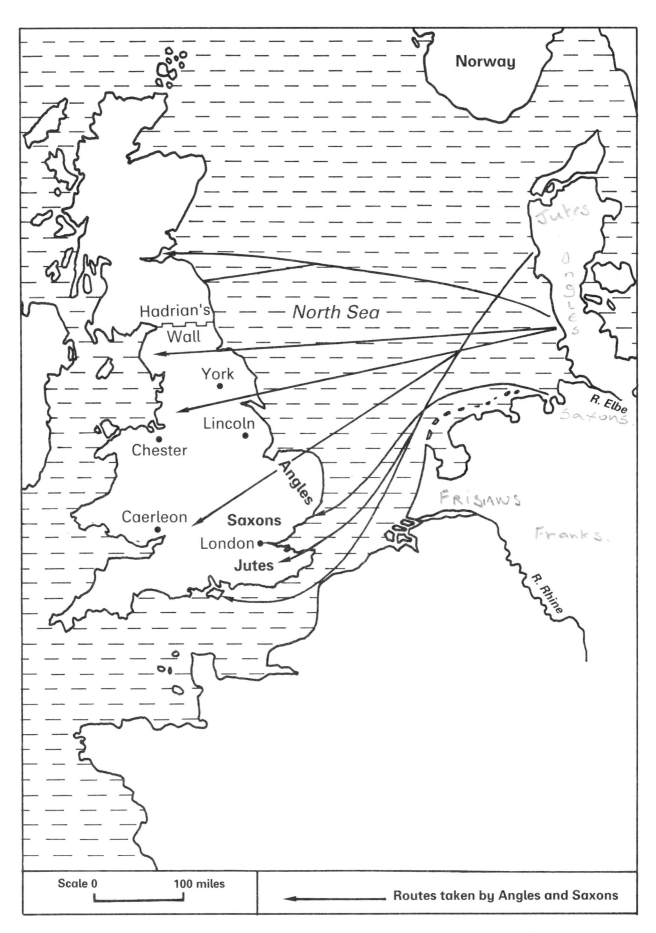

Scale 0   100 miles

⟵——————— Routes taken by Angles and Saxons

Name: _____

Anglo-Saxon Britain

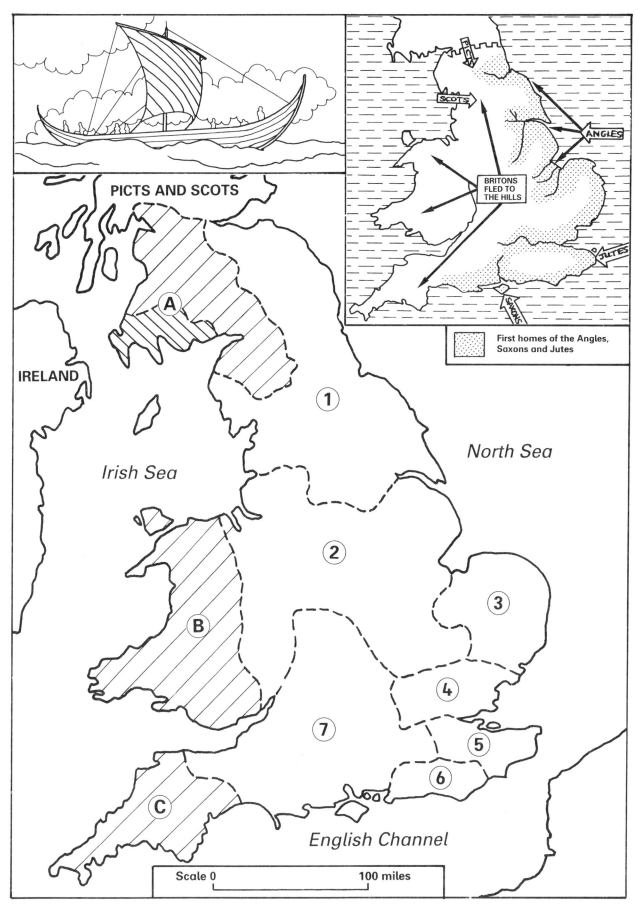

PICTS AND SCOTS

IRELAND

A

Irish Sea

B

C

1

2

3

4

5

6

7

North Sea

English Channel

Scale 0   100 miles

First homes of the Angles,
Saxons and Jutes

Name: _____

King Arthur

MERLIN

THE HOLY GRAIL

KING ARTHUR

EXCALIBUR

QUEEN GUINEVERE

MORDRED

LANCELOT

The three-field system

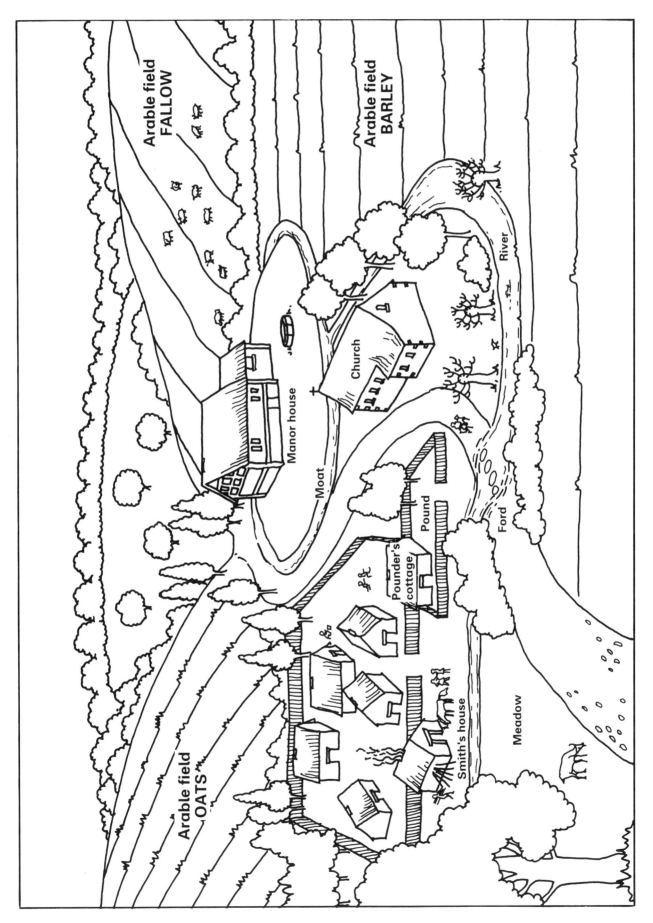

The thane and his lady

Venerable Bede

Name: _____

Illuminated writing

Name: _____

At home with the Anglo-Saxons

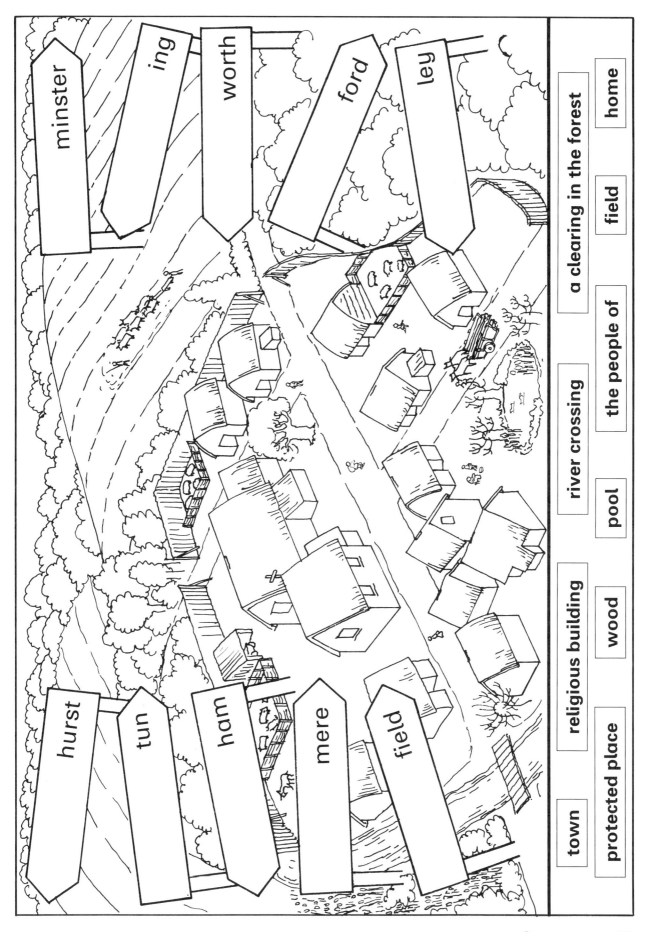

minster

ing

worth

ford

ley

hurst

tun

ham

mere

field

a clearing in the forest

home

field

the people of

river crossing

pool

religious building

wood

town

protected place

Off to England

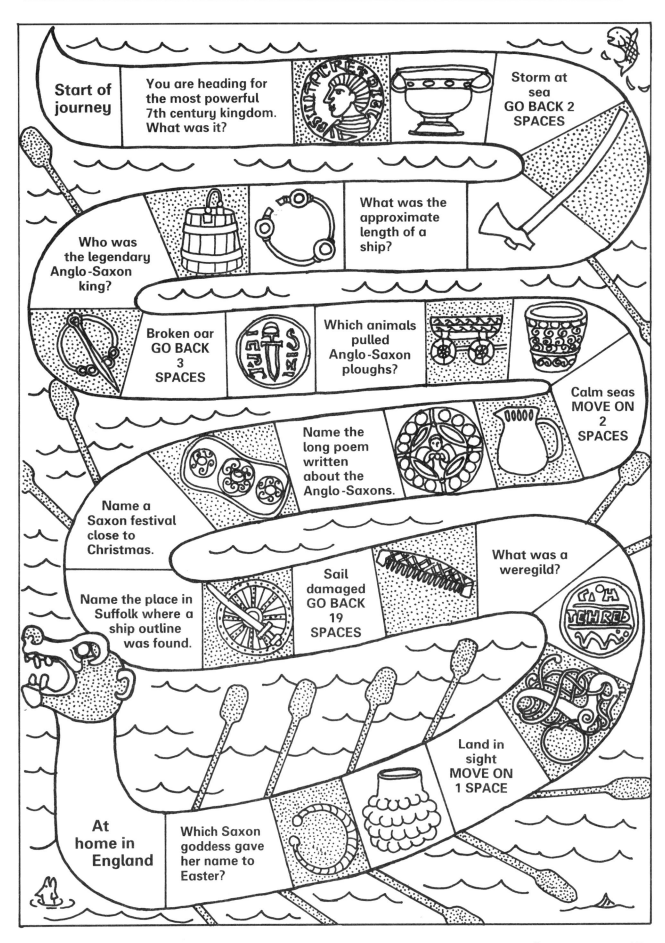

Start of journey

You are heading for the most powerful 7th century kingdom. What was it?

Storm at sea GO BACK 2 SPACES

Who was the legendary Anglo-Saxon king?

What was the approximate length of a ship?

Broken oar GO BACK 3 SPACES

Which animals pulled Anglo-Saxon ploughs?

Calm seas MOVE ON 2 SPACES

Name the long poem written about the Anglo-Saxons.

Name a Saxon festival close to Christmas.

Name the place in Suffolk where a ship outline was found.

Sail damaged GO BACK 19 SPACES

What was a weregild?

Land in sight MOVE ON 1 SPACE

At home in England

Which Saxon goddess gave her name to Easter?

Copymaster 18

Name: _____

The seven Saxon kingdoms of Britain

Territories of the Britons

Territories of the Picts or of the Picts and Scots

Strathclyde

Galloway

Cumbria

Ireland

North Sea

Northumbria

Irish Sea

Mercia

East Anglia

North Wales

Essex

Wessex

Kent

Sussex

West Wales

English Channel

Scale 0   100 miles

Name: _____

Journeys of the Norse seafarers

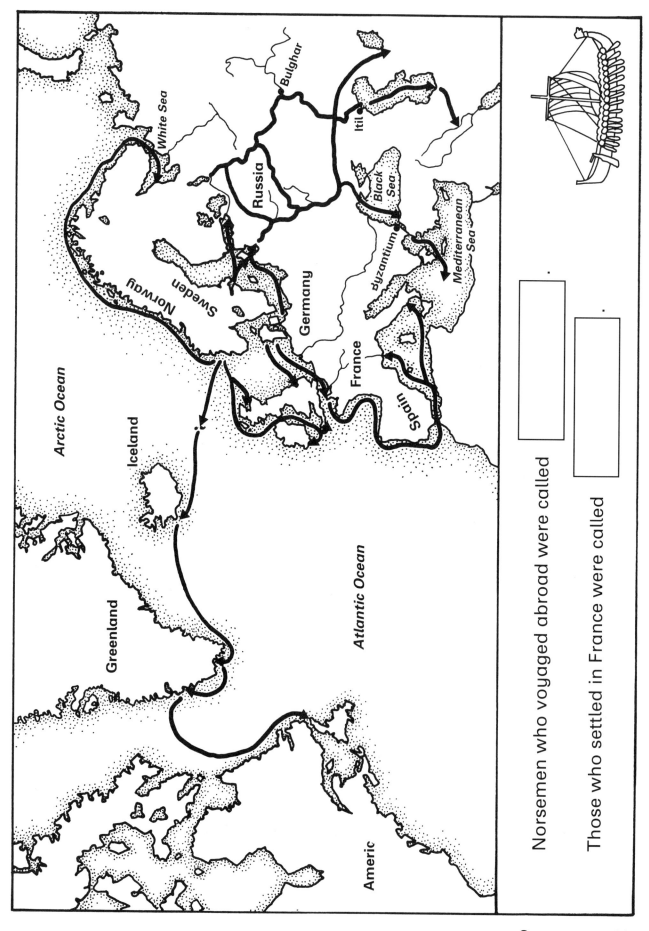

Norsemen who voyaged abroad were called

Those who settled in France were called

A Viking trader/warrior

Serpent of the sea

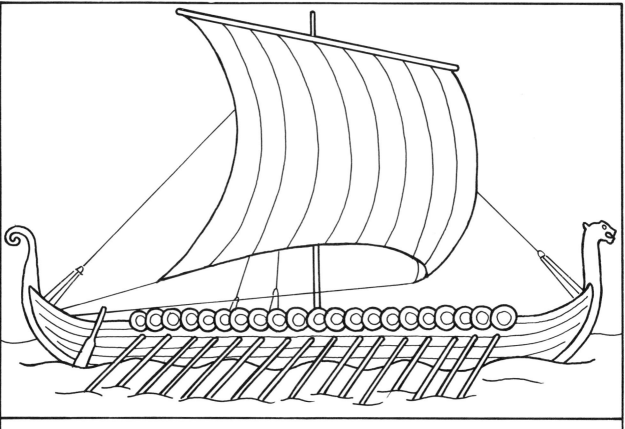

Vikings were the first European people to build ships with

[   ] . The ships had carved [   ] at the

front in the shapes of animals. They were made of strong [   ]

wood. They were steered by large [   ] . Their sails were

[   ] in shape.

A Viking house

Name: _____

Beowulf

Beowulf fought the monster, Grendel.
Complete this picture and colour it.

Odin and other Viking gods

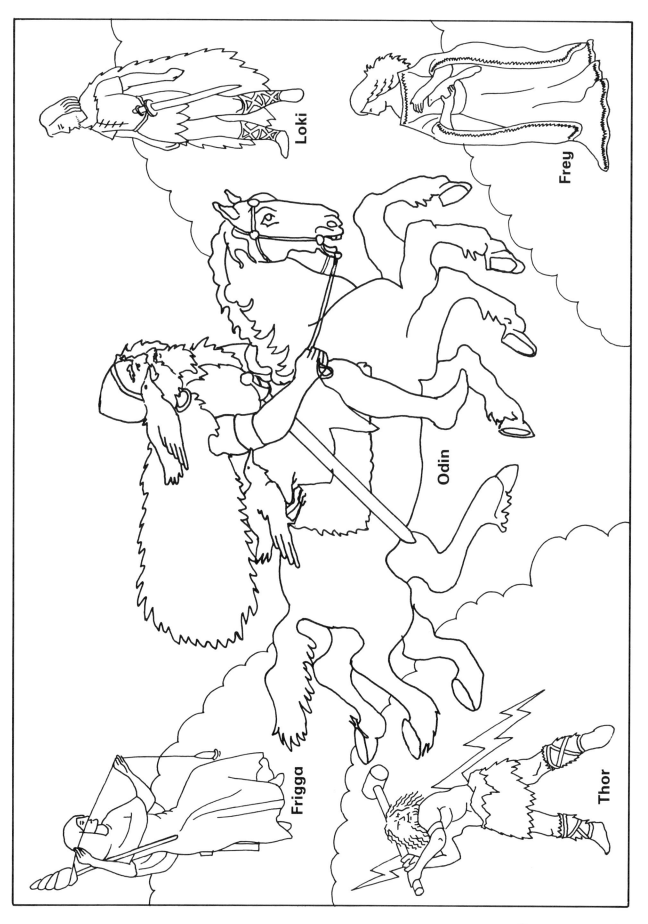

Name: _____

Runes

Viking letters were called runes.

Runes were made up of [_____] lines.

They were [_____] on stone or wood.

This alphabet has [____] letters.

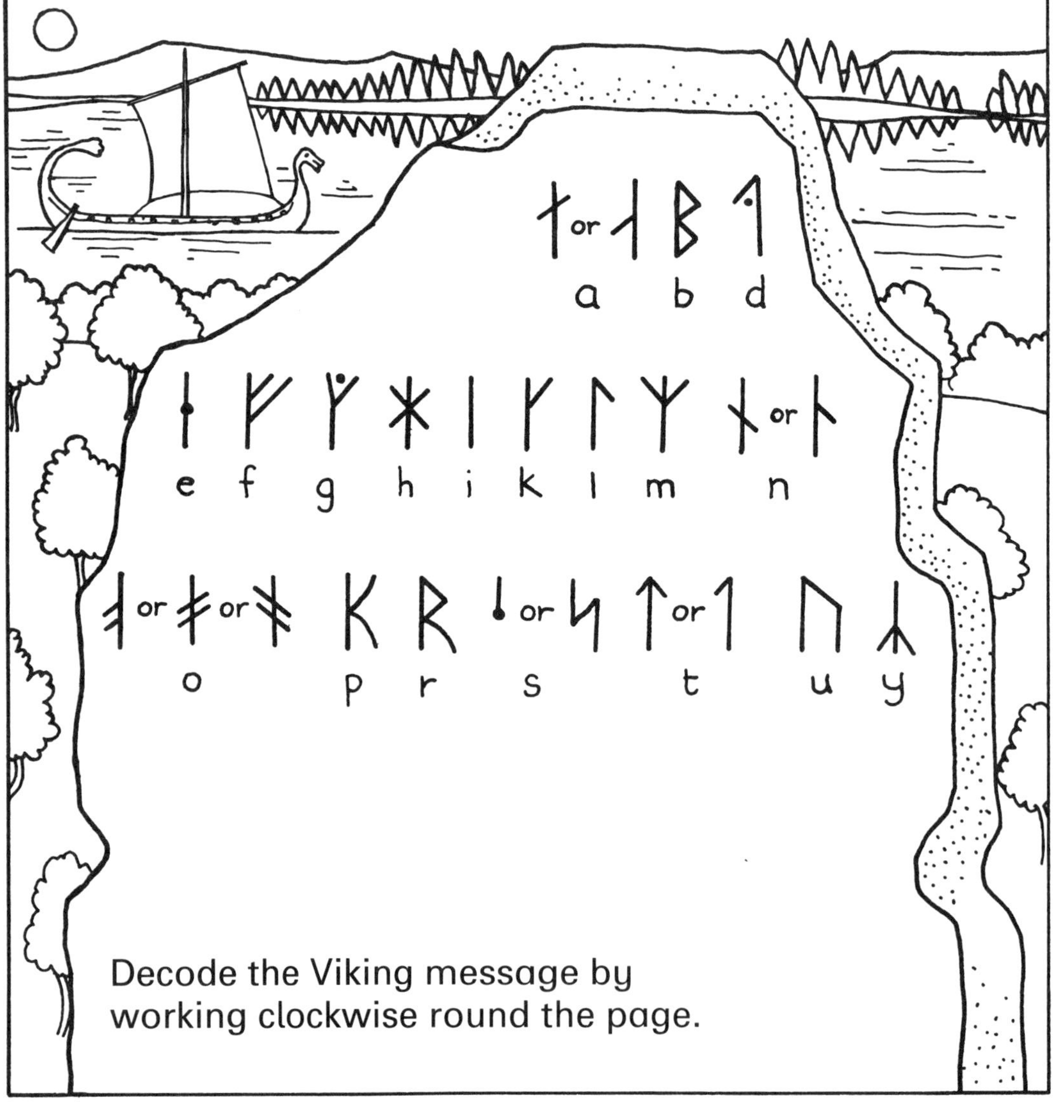

rune	a
† or ↑	a
B	b
↑	d

e f g h i k l m n

o p r s t u y

Decode the Viking message by working clockwise round the page.

Name: _____

Dates to remember

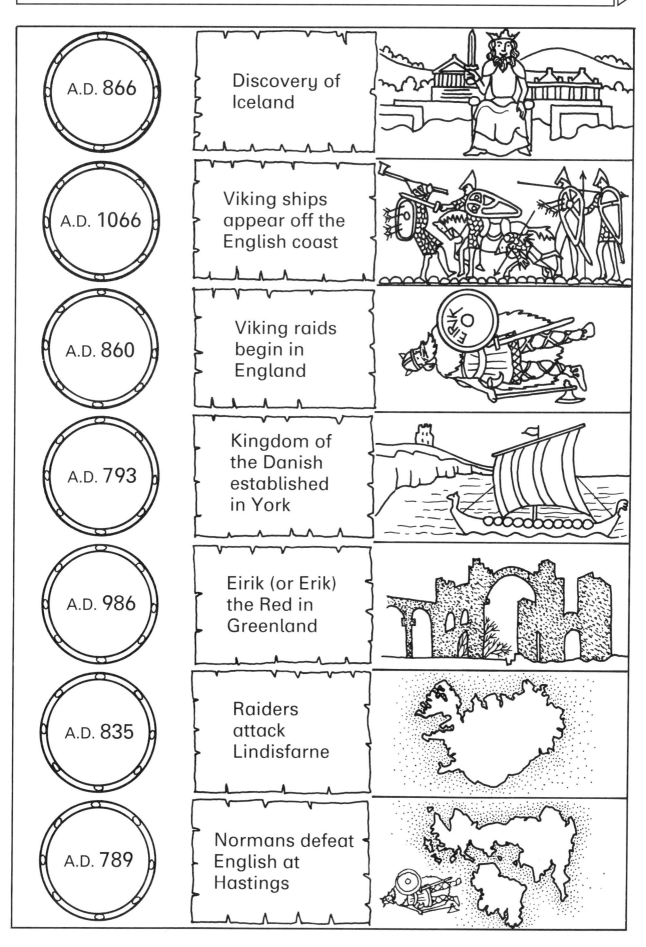

A.D. 866	Discovery of Iceland	
A.D. 1066	Viking ships appear off the English coast	
A.D. 860	Viking raids begin in England	
A.D. 793	Kingdom of the Danish established in York	
A.D. 986	Eirik (or Erik) the Red in Greenland	
A.D. 835	Raiders attack Lindisfarne	
A.D. 789	Normans defeat English at Hastings	

The Tudor Family tree

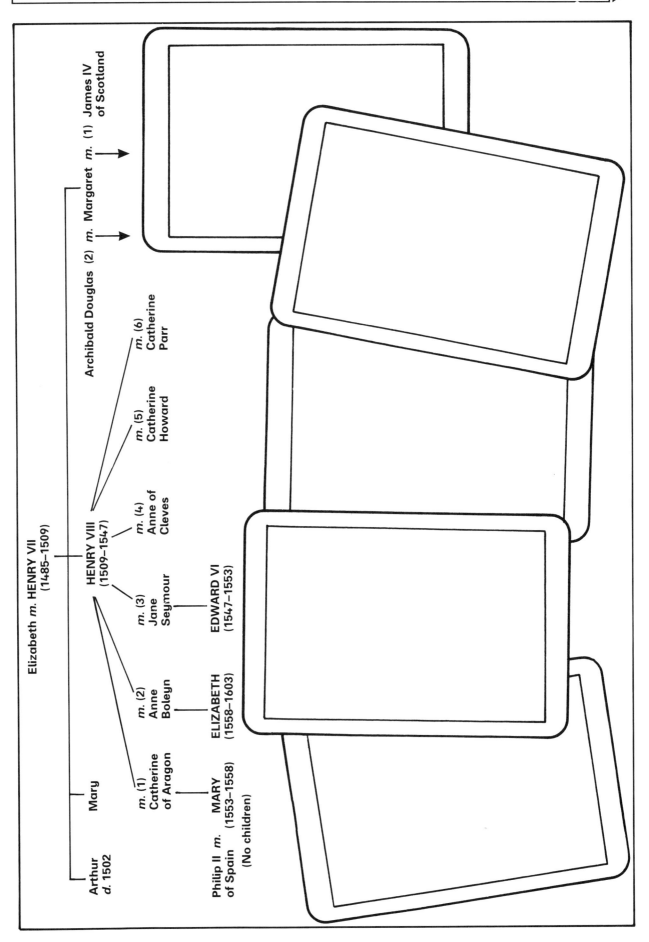

Elizabeth *m.* **HENRY VII**
(1485–1509)

Arthur
d. 1502

Mary

m. (1)
Catherine
of Aragon

MARY (1553–1558)
Philip II *m.*
of Spain
(No children)

m. (2)
Anne
Boleyn

ELIZABETH
(1558–1603)

m. (3)
Jane
Seymour

EDWARD VI
(1547–1553)

HENRY VIII
(1509–1547)

m. (4)
Anne of
Cleves

m. (5)
Catherine
Howard

m. (6)
Catherine
Parr

Margaret *m.* (1) James IV
of Scotland

Archibald Douglas (2) *m.*

A Tudor timeline

Events

Date
1485
1488
1492
1509
1534
1536
1547
1549
1553
1559
1562
1564
1587
1588
1603

Name: _____

The *Mary Rose*

Queen Elizabeth I

Name: _____

The Spanish Armada

galleons,   fleet,   tactics,   Cadiz,   tempestuous,   Armada

Name: _____

Thomas More

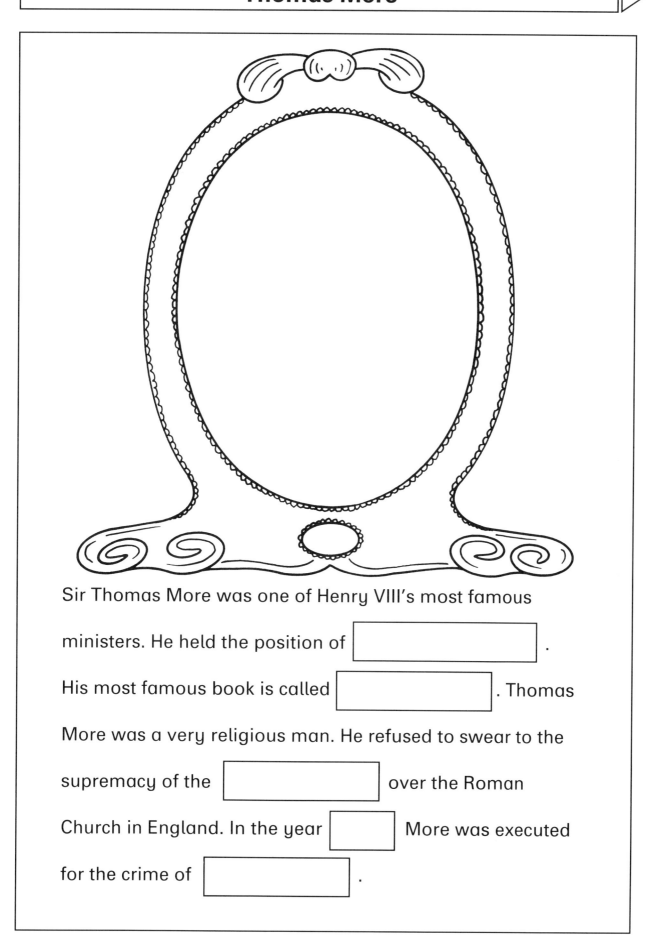

Sir Thomas More was one of Henry VIII's most famous

ministers. He held the position of [   ].

His most famous book is called [   ]. Thomas

More was a very religious man. He refused to swear to the

supremacy of the [   ] over the Roman

Church in England. In the year [   ] More was executed

for the crime of [   ].

Name: _____

Can you reach the fountain?

Name: _____

Shakespeare's Globe Theatre

Where was Shakespeare born? Where is he buried?
Who was his wife?
What kinds of plays did he write?

Name: _____

Queen Victoria

1837   1901

Queen Victoria reigned for longer than any other

English monarch. She ruled for ☐ years,

and died at the age of ☐ on 22 January ☐ .

Name: _____

Chief industrial centres in 1860

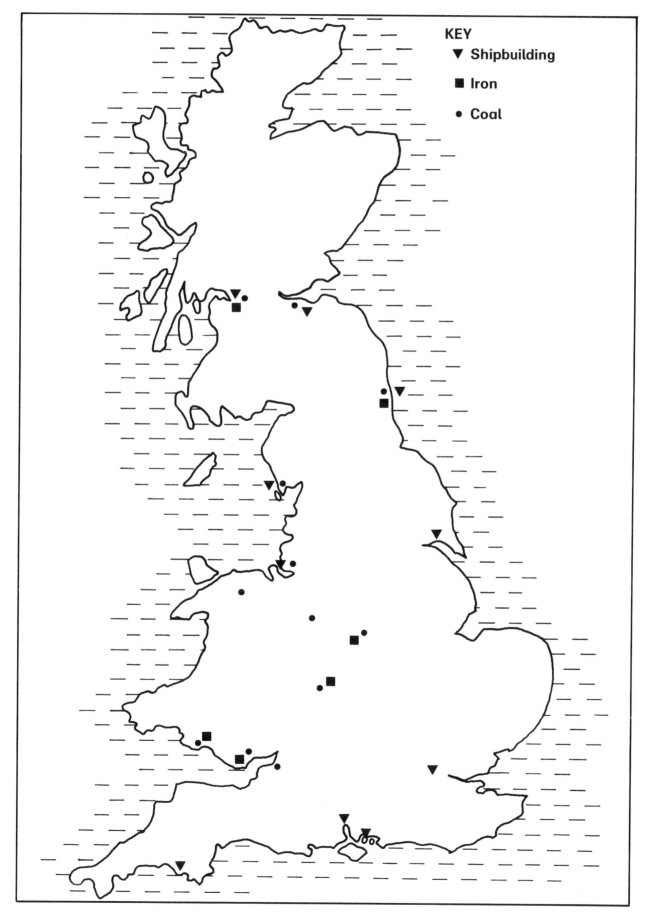

KEY

▼ Shipbuilding

■ Iron

• Coal

Name: _____

Working children

Some children worked

in _____.

Other children worked

in _____.

These children carried

_____ loads all day.

This boy had to

_____.

How old were many children
when they went to work?

_____

How many hours a day
did children often have

to work? _____

How did Doctor Barnardo try to help poor children?

_____

_____

The workhouse game

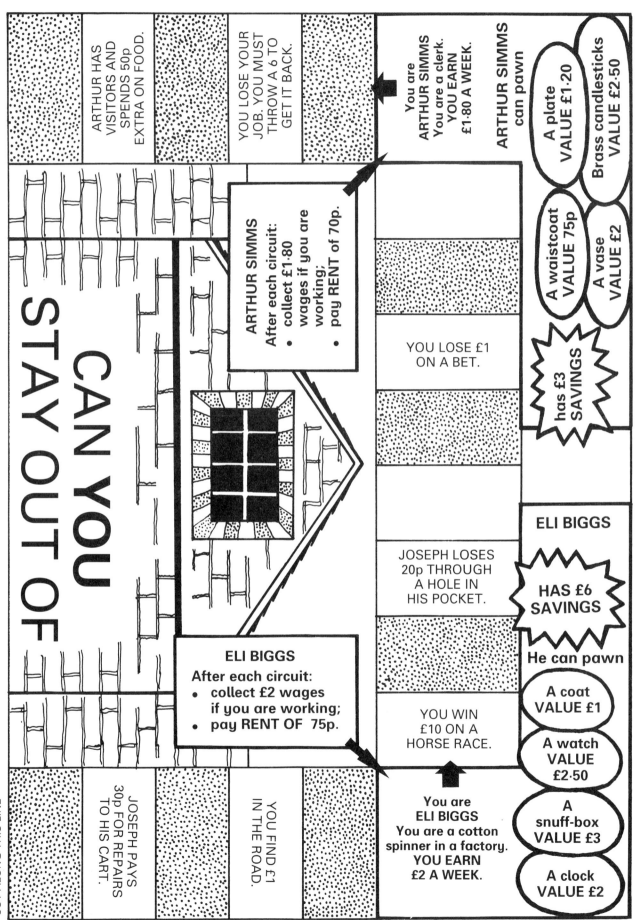

CAN YOU STAY OUT OF

ARTHUR HAS VISITORS AND SPENDS 50p EXTRA ON FOOD.

YOU LOSE YOUR JOB. YOU MUST THROW A 6 TO GET IT BACK.

You are ARTHUR SIMMS
You are a clerk.
YOU EARN £1·80 A WEEK.

ARTHUR SIMMS can pawn

A plate VALUE £1·20

Brass candlesticks VALUE £2·50

A waistcoat VALUE 75p

A vase VALUE £2

has £3 SAVINGS

ARTHUR SIMMS
After each circuit:
• collect £1·80 wages if you are working;
• pay RENT of 70p.

YOU LOSE £1 ON A BET.

JOSEPH LOSES 20p THROUGH A HOLE IN HIS POCKET.

ELI BIGGS

HAS £6 SAVINGS

He can pawn

A coat VALUE £1

A watch VALUE £2·50

A snuff-box VALUE £3

A clock VALUE £2

ELI BIGGS
After each circuit:
• collect £2 wages if you are working;
• pay RENT OF 75p.

YOU WIN £10 ON A HORSE RACE.

You are ELI BIGGS
You are a cotton spinner in a factory.
YOU EARN £2 A WEEK.

JOSEPH PAYS 30p FOR REPAIRS TO HIS CART.

YOU FIND £1 IN THE ROAD.

CUT ALONG THIS LINE

The workhouse game

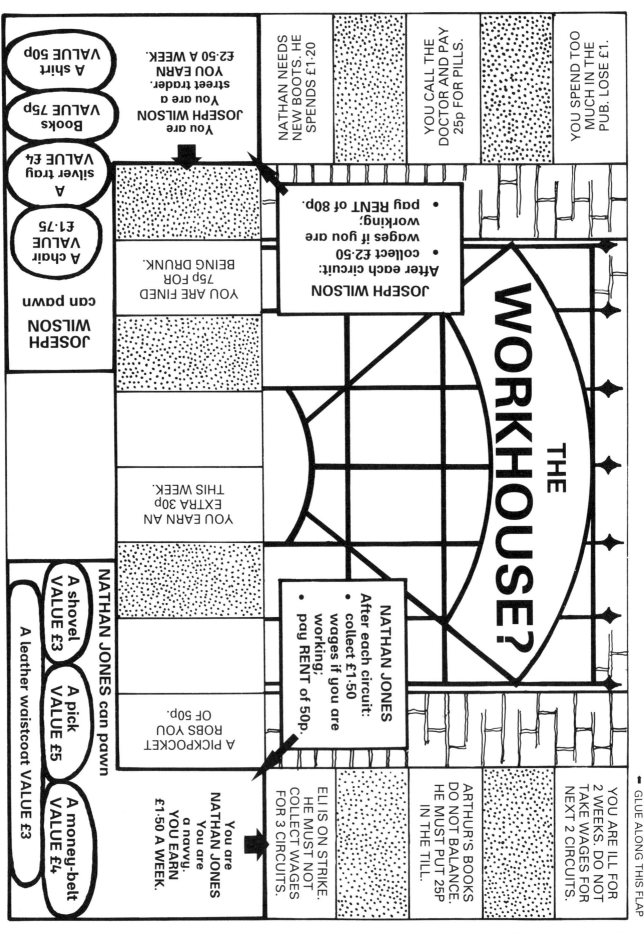

A shirt VALUE 50p

Books VALUE 75p

A silver tray VALUE £4

A chair VALUE £1.75

JOSEPH WILSON can pawn

You are JOSEPH WILSON
You are a street trader.
YOU EARN £2.50 A WEEK.

YOU ARE FINED 75p FOR BEING DRUNK.

JOSEPH WILSON
After each circuit:
• collect £2.50 wages if you are working;
• pay RENT of 80p.

NATHAN NEEDS NEW BOOTS. HE SPENDS £1.20

YOU CALL THE DOCTOR AND PAY 25p FOR PILLS.

YOU SPEND TOO MUCH IN THE PUB. LOSE £1.

THE WORKHOUSE?

YOU EARN AN EXTRA 30p THIS WEEK.

A shovel VALUE £3

A pick VALUE £5

A money-belt VALUE £4

NATHAN JONES can pawn

A leather waistcoat VALUE £3

NATHAN JONES
After each circuit:
• collect £1·50 wages if you are working;
• pay RENT of 50p.

A PICKPOCKET ROBS YOU OF 50p.

You are NATHAN JONES
You are a navvy.
YOU EARN £1·50 A WEEK.

ELI IS ON STRIKE. HE MUST NOT COLLECT WAGES FOR 3 CIRCUITS.

ARTHUR'S BOOKS DO NOT BALANCE. HE MUST PUT 25P IN THE TILL.

YOU ARE ILL FOR 2 WEEKS. DO NOT TAKE WAGES FOR NEXT 2 CIRCUITS.

GLUE ALONG THIS FLAP

Name: _____

Childhood memories

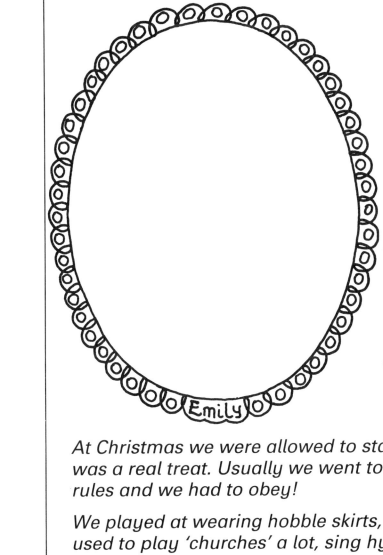

We were not allowed to play on Sundays if we made a noise, and there was no reading of newspapers. We always remembered birthdays and gave one gift – nothing more, nothing less. The first gift I remember was on my fifth birthday, when my Dad gave me Longfellow's poetry book. I was so delighted with it and I learnt some of the poems off by heart, like The Wreck of the Hesperus. *I could recite some of these verses today.*

At Christmas we were allowed to stay up until 9 o'clock, and that was a real treat. Usually we went to bed at 7.30 p.m. Those were rules and we had to obey!

We played at wearing hobble skirts, all tight around our legs. We used to play 'churches' a lot, sing hymns, act them out. We played games like this in the woodshed. I had a really beautiful doll's house with everything upholstered. We also played schools, cards, skipping, jumping and cricket. I could jump over a five-barred gate when I was eleven. I used to like sewing, and dressed dolls for the church fete. They would cost 1s 11d.

The book I remember best is Pilgrim's Progress. *I got it as a prize for being good at school.*

Name: _____

A wealthy Victorian home

Nursery

Bedroom

Drawing-room

Kitchen

Now draw the sort of home
a poor family might have lived in.

Morse Code

A ·—	B —···	C —·—·	D —··	E ·	F ··—·
G —··	H ····	I ··	J ·———	K —·—	L ·—··
M ——	N —·	O ———	P ·——·	Q ——·—	R ·—·
S ···	T —	U ··—	V ···—	W ·——	X —··—
Y —·——	Z ——··	FULL STOP ·—·—·—			
1 ·————	2 ··———	3 ···——	4 ····—	5 ·····	6 —····
7 ——···	8 ———··	9 ————·	0 —————		

My name is

Name: _____

The Great Exhibition

Name: _____

Victorian dress

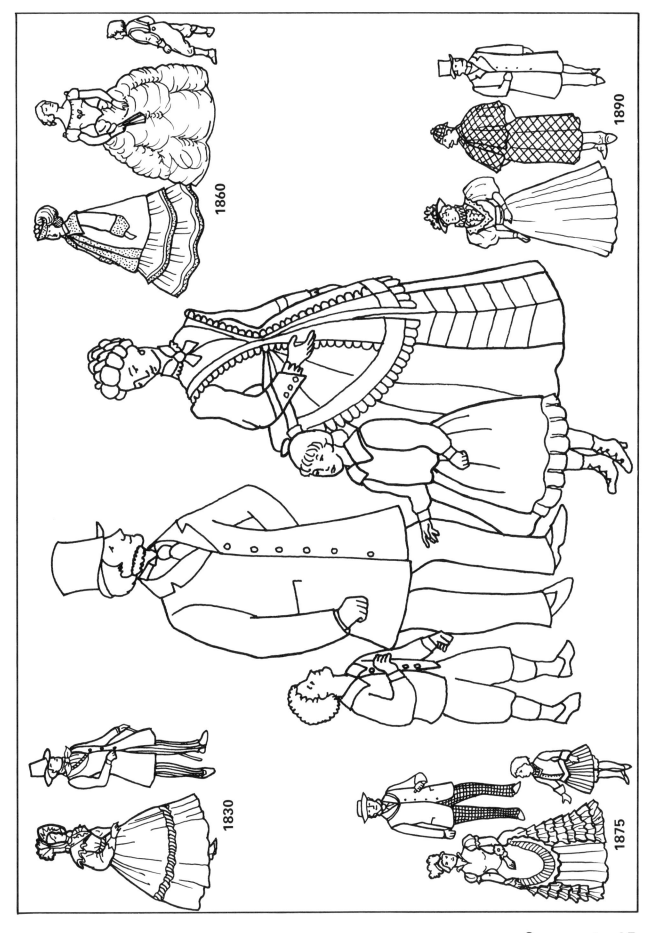

Name: _____

The British Empire 1914

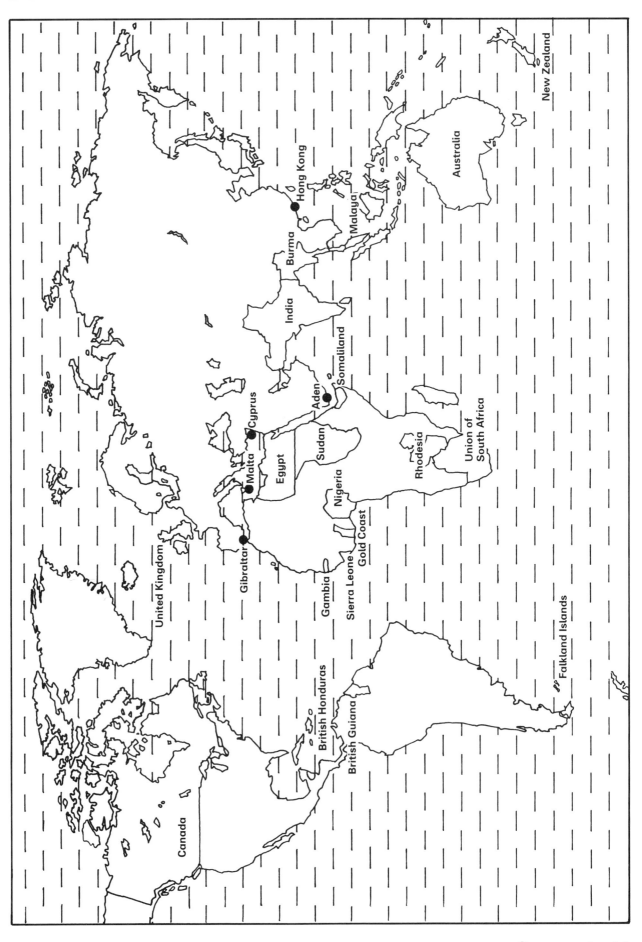

New Zealand

Australia

Hong Kong

Burma

Malaya

India

Somaliland

Aden

Cyprus

Sudan

Union of
South Africa

Malta

Egypt

Rhodesia

Nigeria

United Kingdom

Gibraltar

Gold Coast

Gambia

Sierra Leone

Falkland Islands

British Honduras

British Guiana

Canada

The decline of the Empire

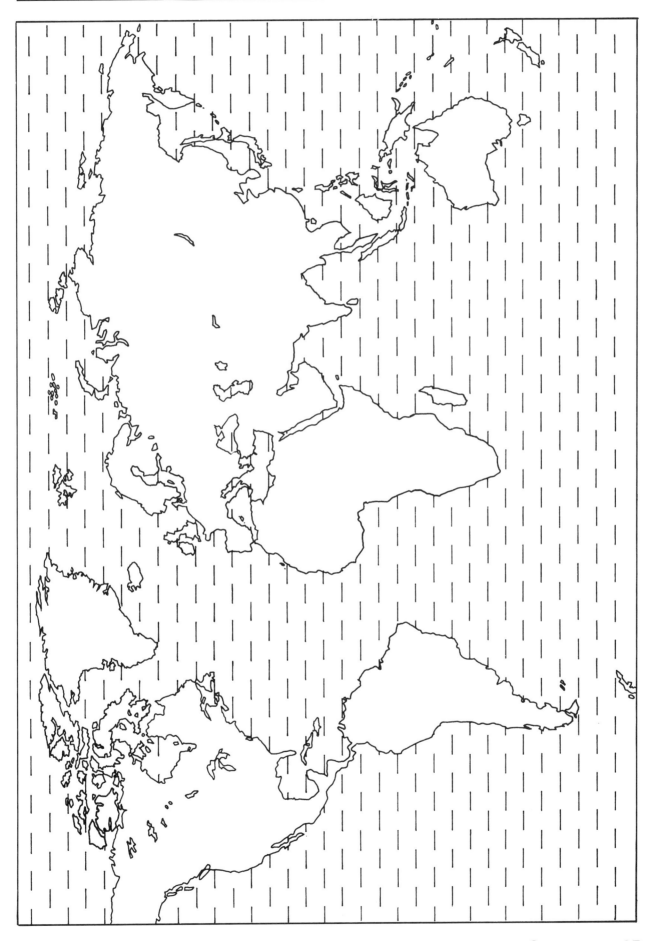

Fighting for Britain

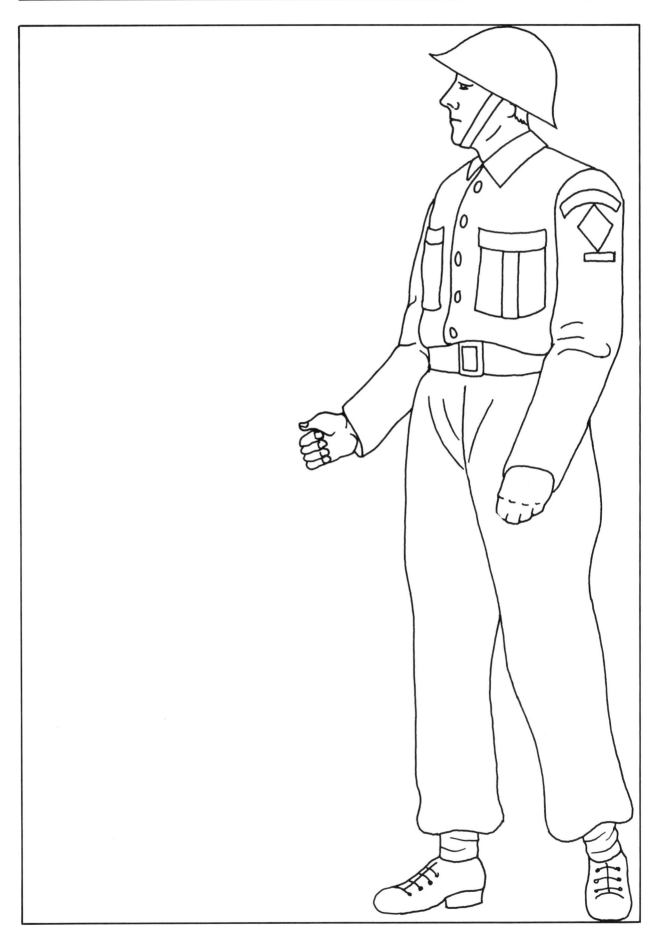

Name: _____

War-time posters

The Squander Bug was said to be helping Hitler if he could

persuade people to _____ their _____ instead of

buying _____ Bonds. He was covered with signs called

_____ to show whose side he was on.

Name: _____

Women at war

Interviews

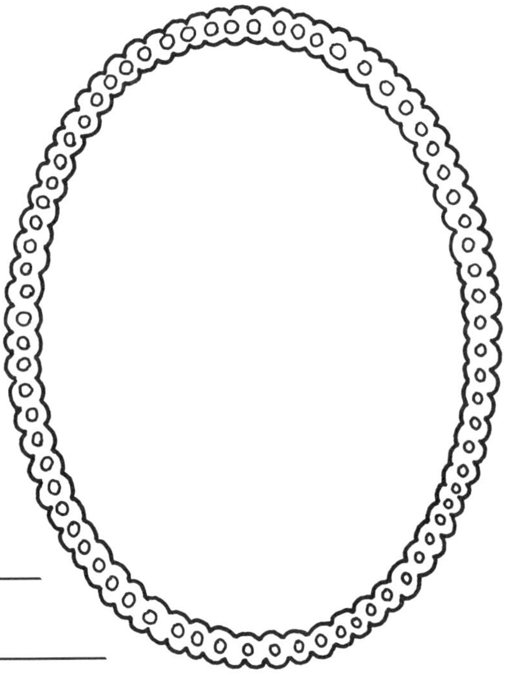

1 When and where were
   you born?

   _____

   _____

2 What was the house like
   that you grew up in?

   _____

   _____

   _____

   _____

3 Did your mother and father work?
   If so, what did they do? _____

   _____

4 What were your favourite meals
   when you were my age? _____

   _____

   _____

5 What games or toys
   did you like to play or use? _____

   _____

   _____

Name: _____

Matters for concern

A timeline since 1930

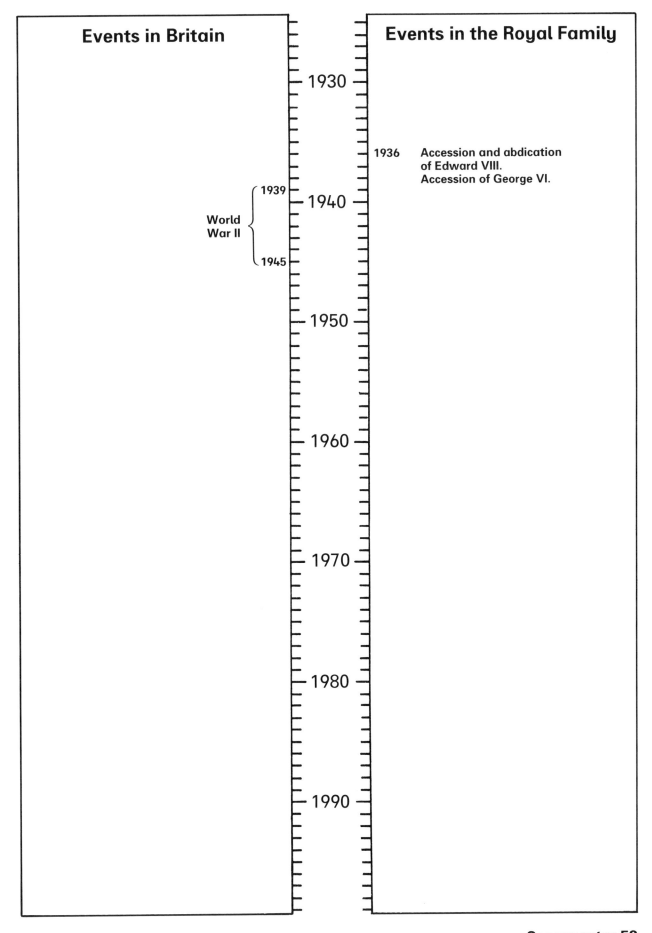

Events in Britain

Events in the Royal Family

1930

1936   **Accession and abdication of Edward VIII. Accession of George VI.**

1939 ⎫
⎬ World War II
1945 ⎭

1940

1950

1960

1970

1980

1990

The mighty Wurlitzer

WURLITZER

1	11
2	12
3	13
4	14
5	15
6	16
7	17
8	18
9	19
10	20

Name: _____

Where is Greece?

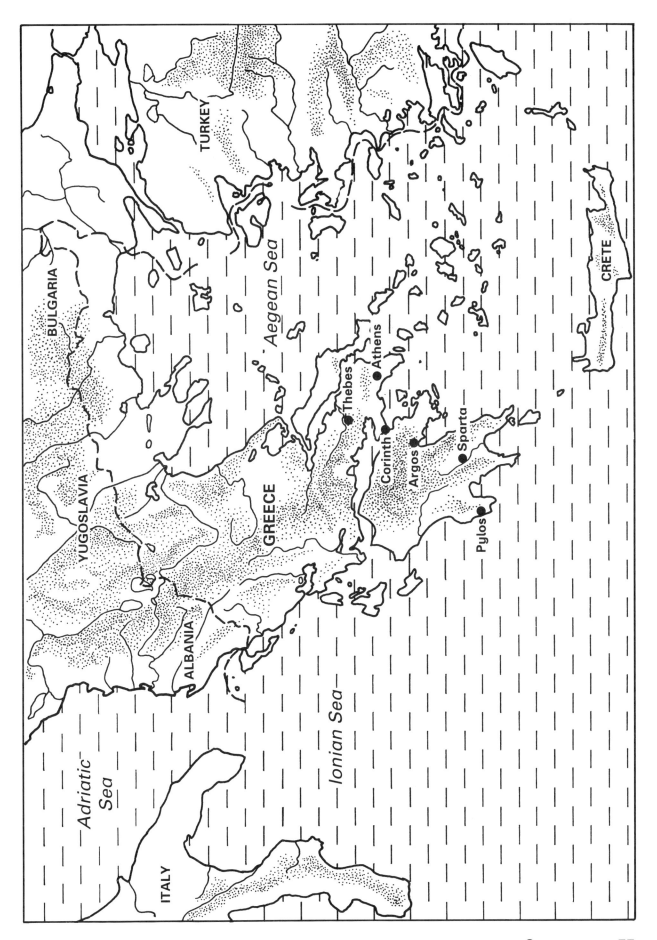

At home in Athens

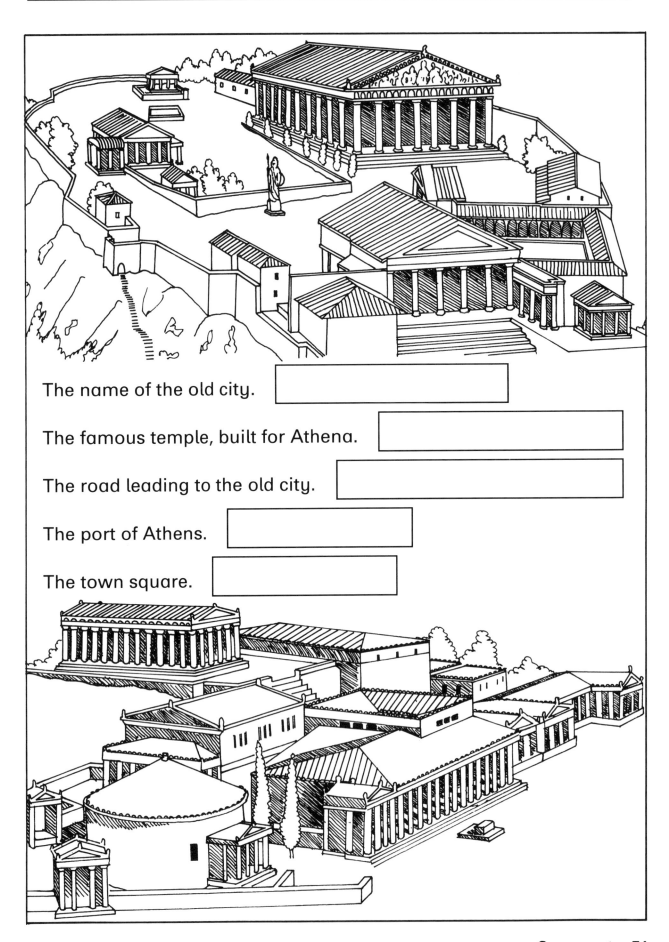

The name of the old city.

The famous temple, built for Athena.

The road leading to the old city.

The port of Athens.

The town square.

Guilty or not guilty

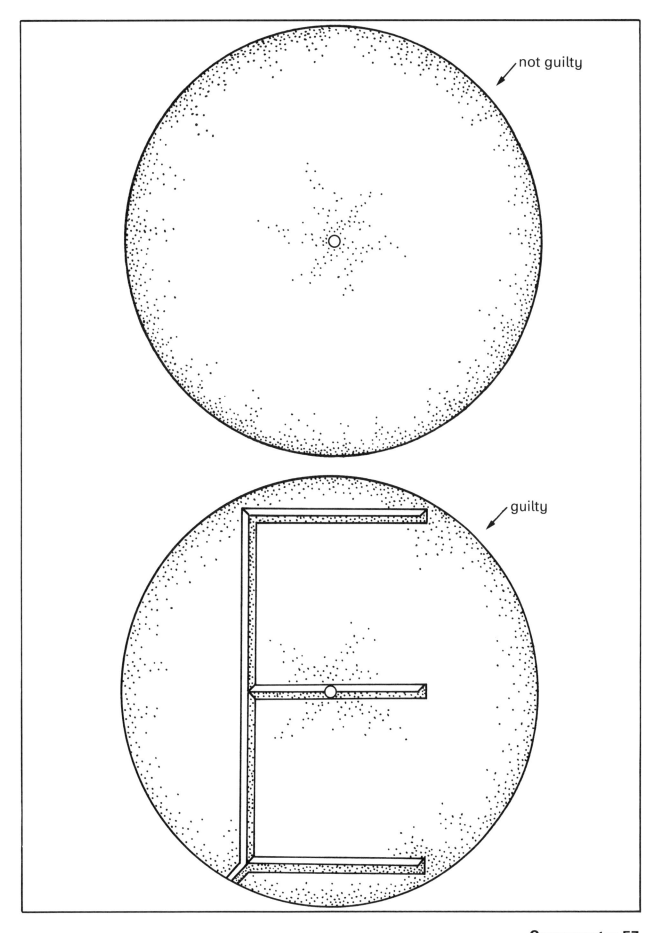

not guilty

guilty

Name: _____

Everyday life in the country

Clues down

1 A Greek farm-worker (8).
2 Fruit for wine (6).
3 Common cereal crop (6).
4 These are harvested for grapes (5).

Clues across

1 An implement for breaking up the soil (6).
2 A method of sowing seeds (12).
3 Trees grown for oil (5).
4 Crops get nutrients from this (4).

Name: _____

The Greek alphabet

$$A \quad B \quad \Gamma \quad \Delta \quad E \quad Z$$

A	B	G	D	E	Z

$$H \quad \Theta \quad I \quad K \quad \Lambda \quad M$$

E	T	I	K	L	M

$$N \quad \Xi \quad O \quad \Pi \quad P \quad \Sigma$$

N	X	O	P	R	S

$$T \quad \Upsilon \quad \Phi \quad X \quad \Psi \quad \Omega$$

T	U	P	C	P	O

Alpha	Beta	Gamma	Delta	Epsilon	Zeta
Eta	Theta	Iota	Kappa	Lambda	Mu
Nu	Xi	Omicron	Pi	Rho	Sigma
Tau	Upsilon	Phi	Chi	Psi	Omega

Masks for the theatre

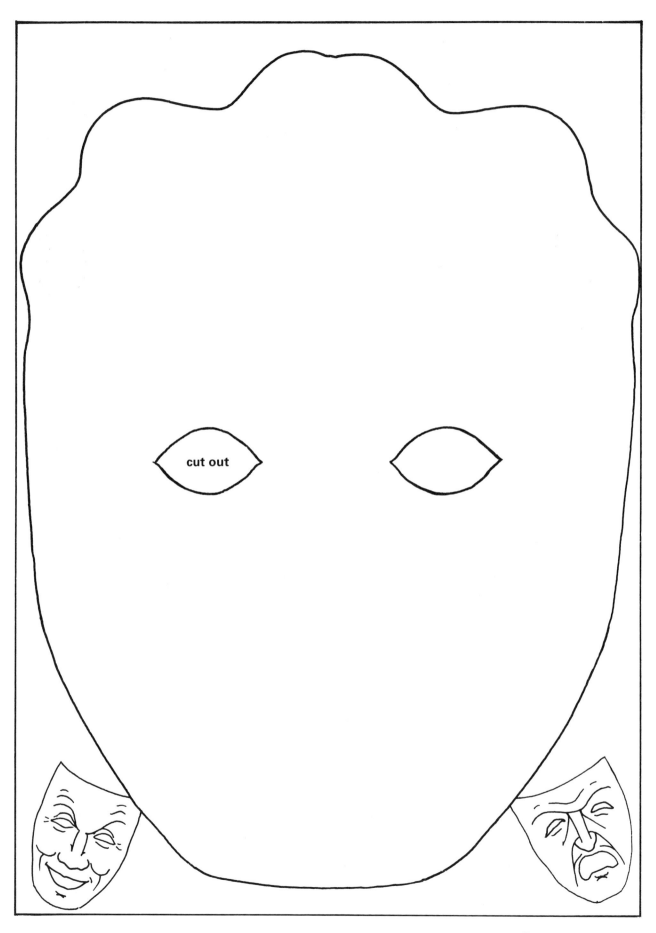

cut out

The Greek Olympic Games

Name: _____

Do you remember?

What is your name? _____

How long have you lived in this country? _____

Do you work or have you worked here? _____

If so, at what? _____

_____

What are the most important changes
you have seen here in your lifetime? _____

_____

_____

_____

Are there things about the area
that have not changed? _____

_____

_____

A dictionary of church architecture

Name of feature	Description	Spotted (tick)
	Places to walk, alongside the chancel or nave.	
	The holy table.	
	The section of the church at the eastern end.	
	The place where the east–west axis of the building is crossed.	
	The main 'body' of the building.	
	The washing basin alongside the altar, used to clean the sacramental vessels.	
	The ornamental screen behind the altar.	
	The transverse section of the building, at 90° to the east–west axis.	

Plan of a parish church

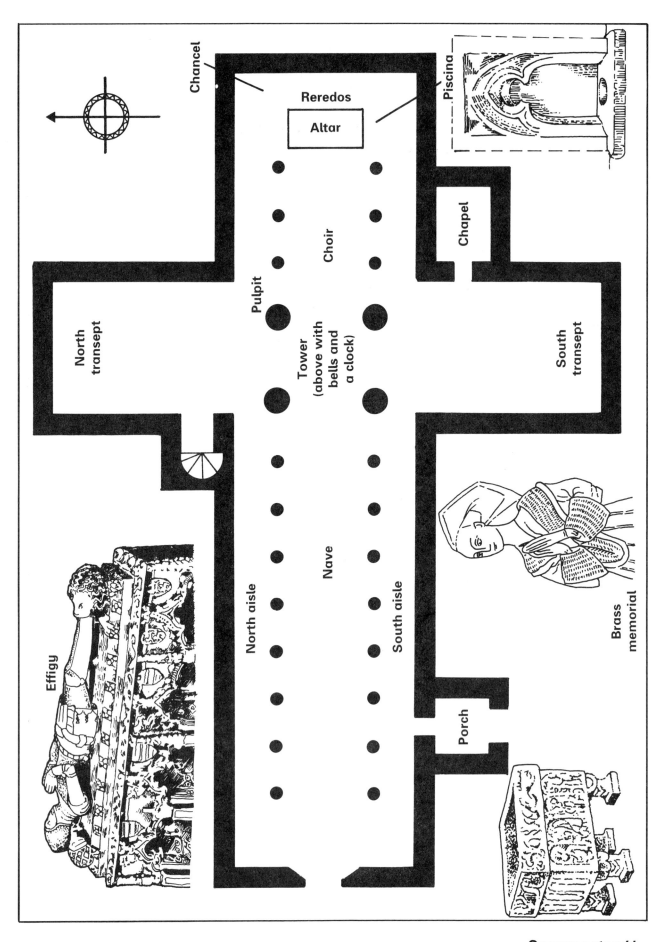

Brass-rubbings

A titled lady of about 1465

A knight of about 1400

13th century armour

14th century armour

Name: _____

Building materials

The church walls are made of _____

Sketch of wall section

The door is made of _____

The roof is made of _____

Name: _____

Gravestones

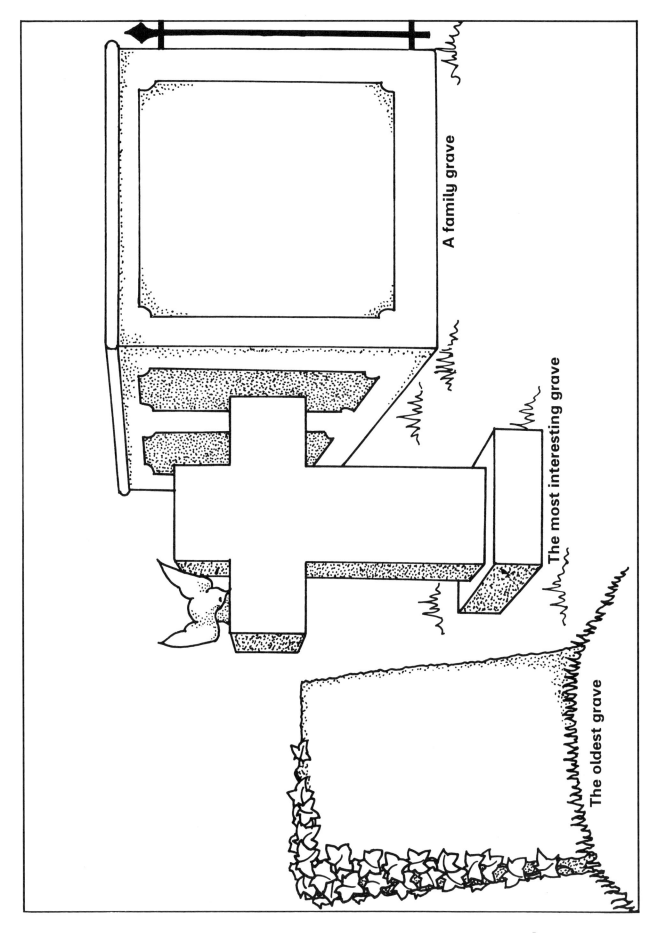

A family grave

The most interesting grave

The oldest grave

Dates to remember

Parish registers had to be kept by law.

1534

1649

1878

1538

800s

597

1285

600s

Payment by tithes became law.

Saint Augustine's mission. Beginning of the Christian church in England.

Start of the church parish system.

Puritans in power under Oliver Cromwell.

William Booth founded the Salvation Army.

Vikings, who worshipped pagan gods, attacked Christians in Britain.

Henry VIII became head of the Church of England.

Copymaster 68

The Egyptian Empire

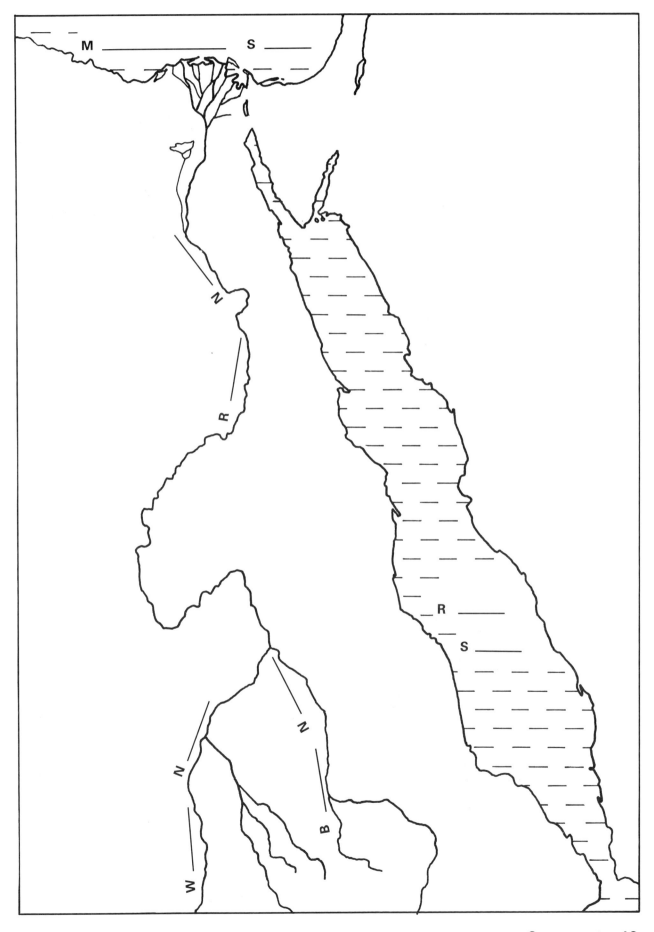

Name: _____

A funeral procession

The pyramid game

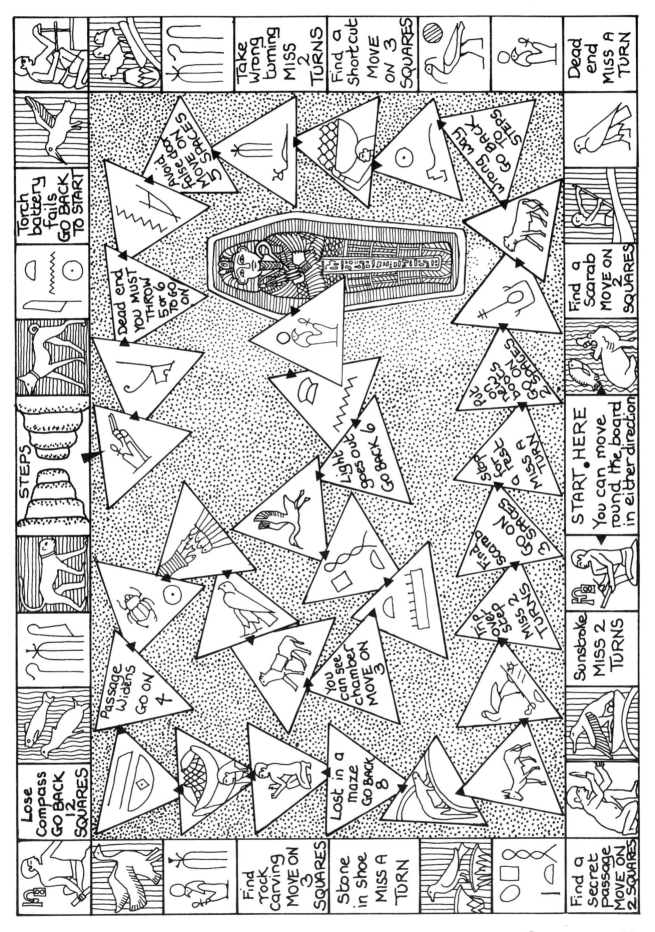

Name: _____

Tutankhamun

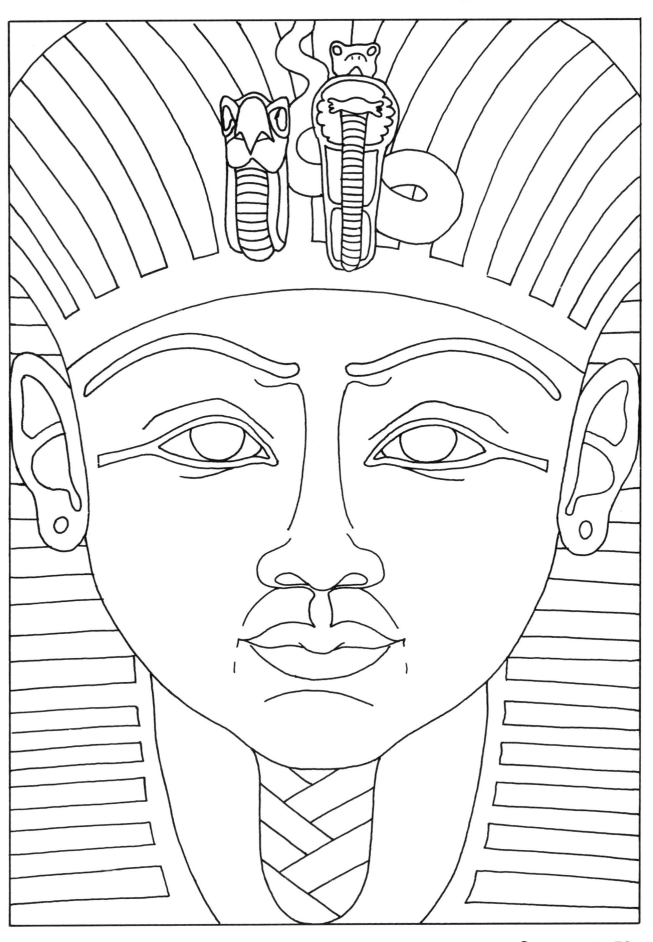

Name: _____

Count like the Egyptians

1	2	3	4	5	6	7	8	9	10
I	II	III	IIII	III II	III III	IIII III	IIII IIII	III III III	∩

20	25	30	100
∩∩	IIII∩∩ II	∩∩∩	𝟗

Find the answers to these Egyptian sums.

III + II =

III + III III =

∩∩ − ∩ =

∩∩ − I∩ =

IIII × III =

II × IIII IIII =

IIII∩∩ − II =

IIIII∩∩ ÷ III III =

∩ + III III − III II =

III∩∩∩ ÷ II∩ III =

II∩∩∩∩ ÷ III III =

Can you write your answers
in Egyptian numbers too?

Name: _____

Hieroglyphics

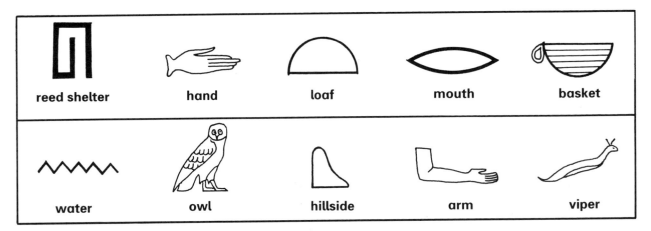

| reed shelter | hand | loaf | mouth | basket |
| water | owl | hillside | arm | viper |

Look through books for other examples of Egyptian writing. Copy the hieroglyphics carefully. Make a list of the symbols that were used in this picture writing.

Name: _____

Gods and goddesses

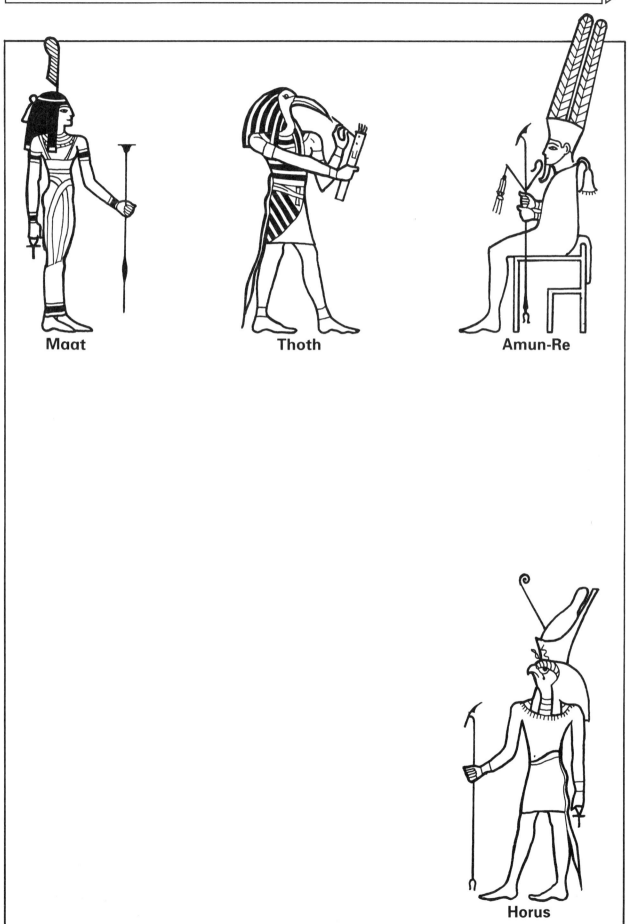

Maat

Thoth

Amun-Re

Horus

Name: _____

Egyptian treasures

Draw a picture of another Egyptian treasure that you would like to discover. Tell the story of how you found it.

Name: _____

Ploughing

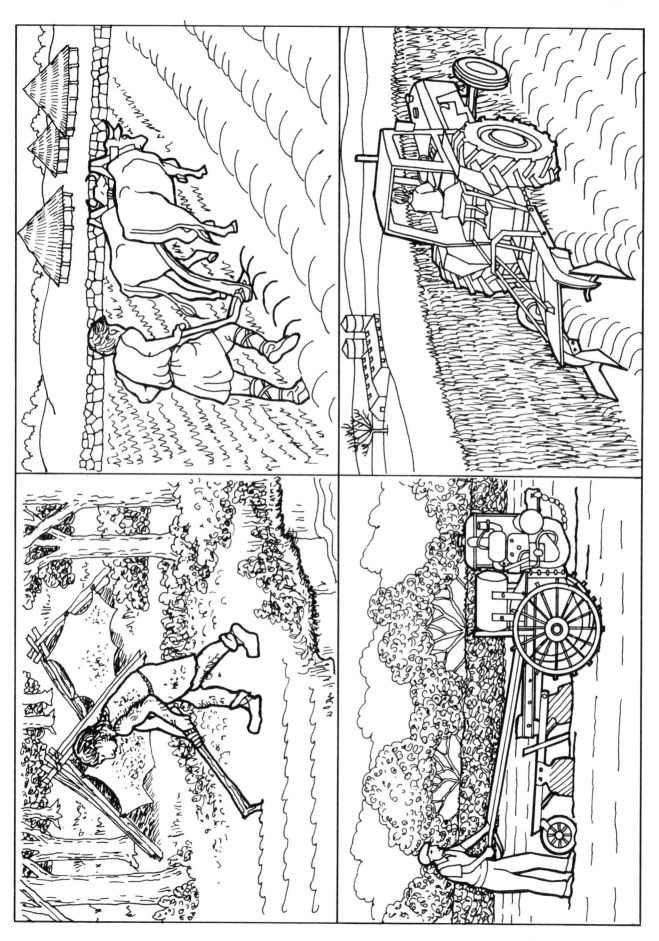

Name: _____

The beginnings of farming

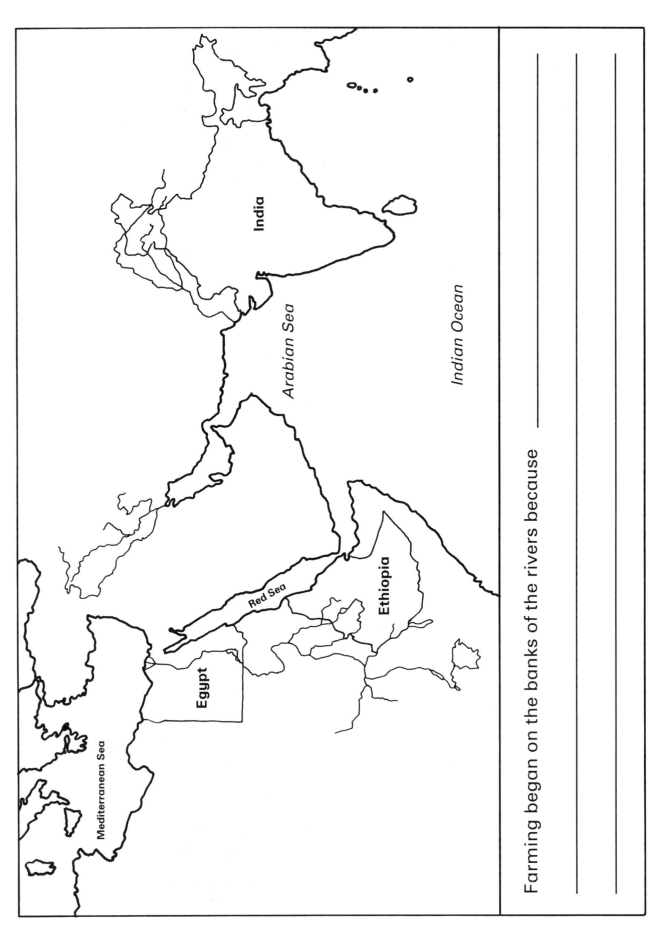

India

Arabian Sea

Indian Ocean

Red Sea

Ethiopia

Egypt

Mediterranean Sea

Farming began on the banks of the rivers because _____

Name: _____

Enclosures

Before enclosures — the three-field system

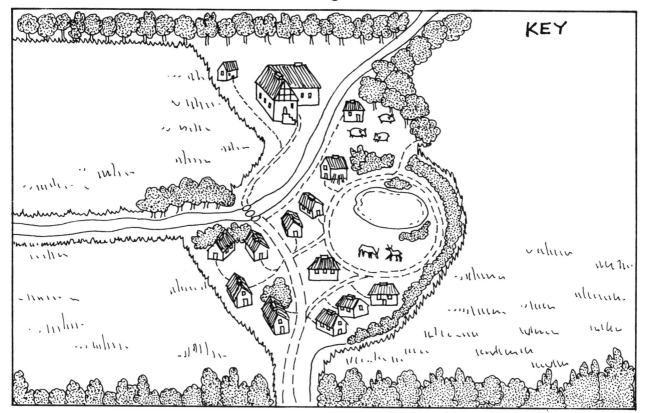

KEY

After enclosures

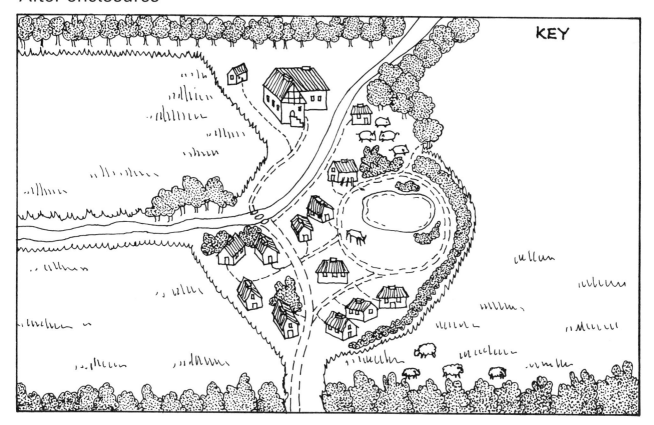

KEY

Name: _____

Four-year rotation

Year 1

Year 2

Year 3

Year 4

KEY ☐ **Turnips** ☐ **Barley** ☐ **Wheat** ☐ **Clover**

Farming around the world

Name: _____

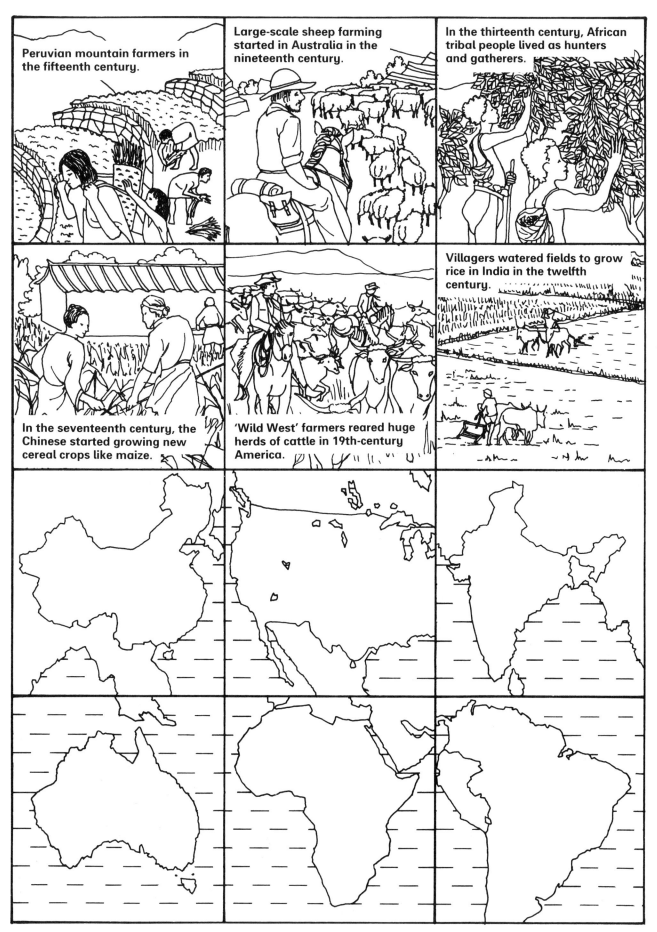

Peruvian mountain farmers in the fifteenth century.

Large-scale sheep farming started in Australia in the nineteenth century.

In the thirteenth century, African tribal people lived as hunters and gatherers.

In the seventeenth century, the Chinese started growing new cereal crops like maize.

'Wild West' farmers reared huge herds of cattle in 19th-century America.

Villagers watered fields to grow rice in India in the twelfth century.

Travelling overland

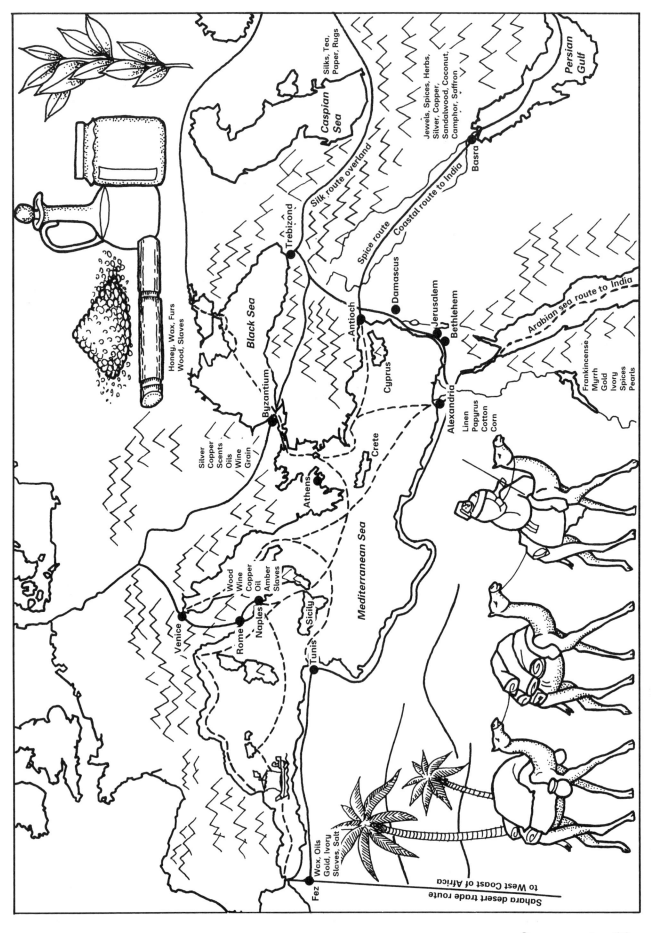

Voyages of exploration

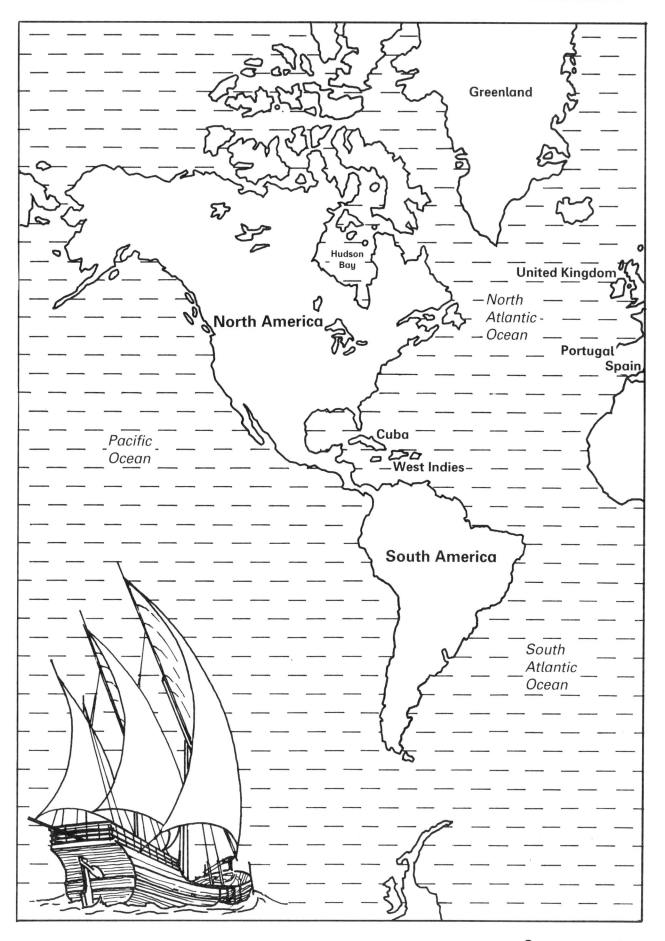

Greenland

North America

Hudson
Bay

United Kingdom

North
Atlantic
Ocean

Portugal
Spain

Pacific
Ocean

Cuba

West Indies

South America

South
Atlantic
Ocean

Voyages of exploration

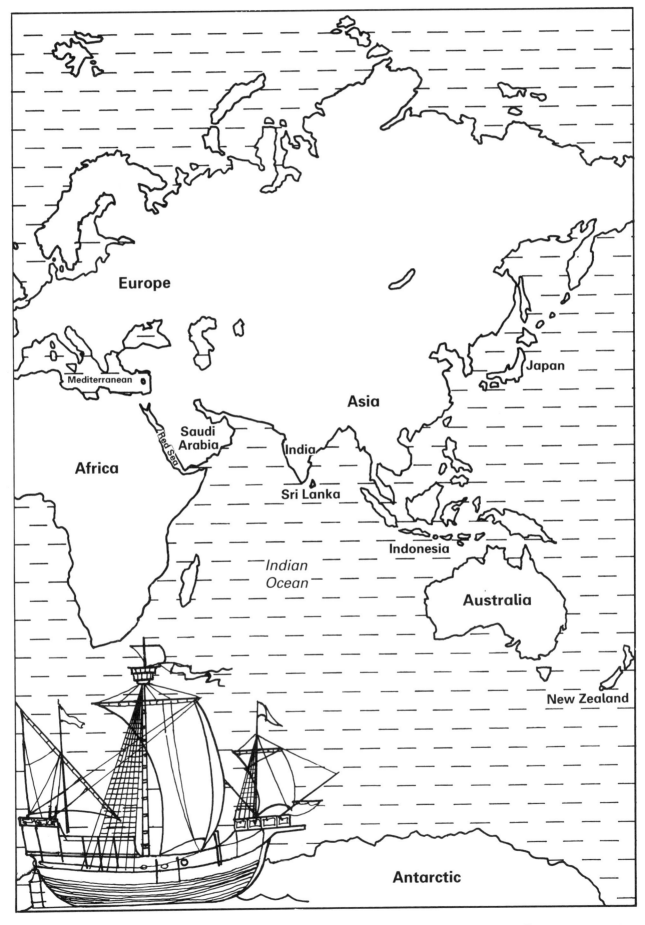

Europe

Mediterranean

Saudi Arabia

Red Sea

Africa

India

Sri Lanka

Asia

Japan

Indonesia

Indian Ocean

Australia

New Zealand

Antarctic

Aids to navigation

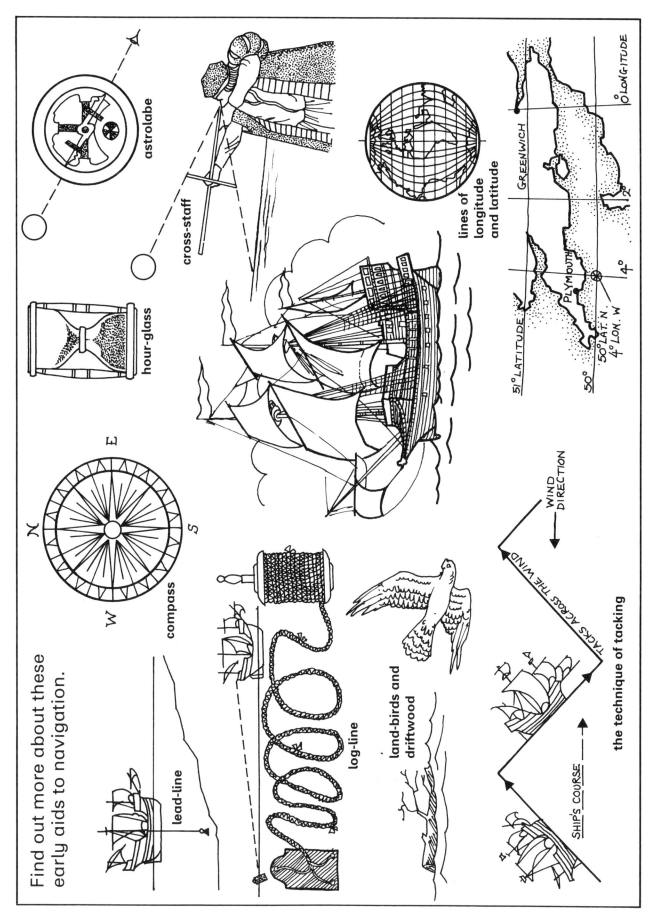

Find out more about these early aids to navigation.

astrolabe

cross-staff

hour-glass

lines of longitude and latitude

GREENWICH

PLYMOUTH

0° LONGITUDE

51° LATITUDE

50°

50° LAT. N.
4° LON. W

4°

compass

N

E

S

W

lead-line

log-line

land-birds and driftwood

WIND DIRECTION

TACKS ACROSS THE WIND

SHIP'S COURSE

the technique of tacking

On board a sailing ship

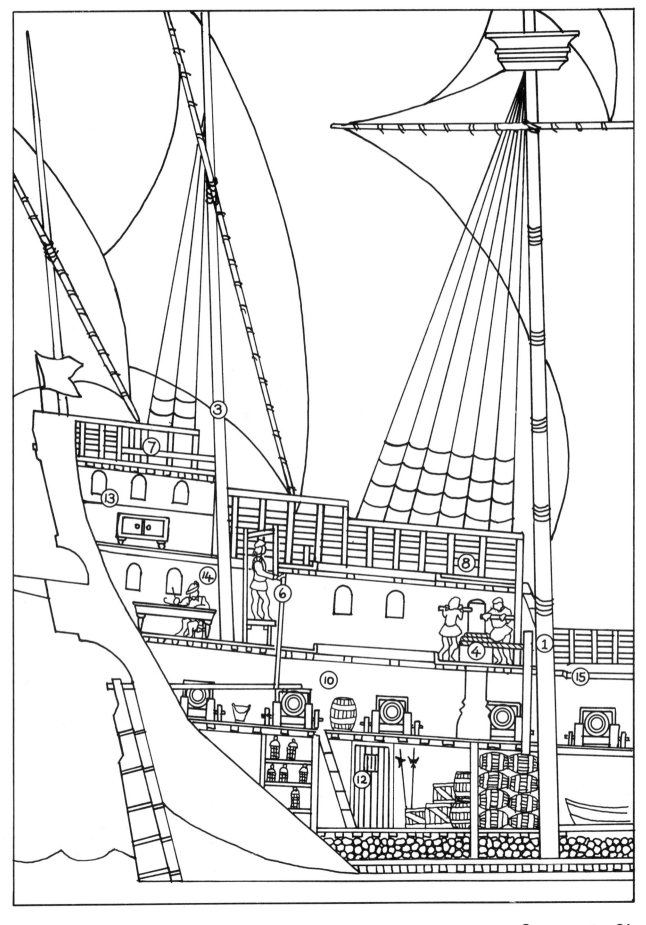

Name: _____

On board a sailing ship

Aztecs and Incas

Aztecs

Incas

North America

KEY

Aztec Empire

Inca Empire

South America

Hernando Cortes

Francisco Pizarro

Aztec warriors

Glyphs

Tenochtitlan

Montezuma

I-spy archaeology

Name: _____

Key dates in world exploration

3500 B.C.	Egyptians known to use boats.
800 B.C.	Homer's *Odyssey* written.
A.D. 800	The Vikings sail to Europe.
1394–1460	Life of Henry the Navigator of Portugal, patron of explorers.
1488	Bartholomew Diaz rounds the Cape of Good Hope (Cape of Storms).
1492	Christopher Columbus reaches the Caribbean, Cuba and Hispaniola.
1497–1499	Vasco da Gama rounds Africa and goes to India.
1519	Ferdinand Magellan's ship sails around the world – the first known circumnavigation of the globe.
1543	The Portuguese arrive in Japan.
1618	Francis Drake makes the second known voyage around the world.
1642–1644	Abel Tasman discovers Tasmania while searching for the 'southern continent'.
1768–1771	Captain James Cook discovers New Zealand.
1785–1788	La Perouse voyages to Asia, North America and the Western Pacific.
1839	Ross tries to reach Antarctica.
1839–1840	Dumont D'Urville goes to Antarctica.
1873	Baron Nordenskjold, a Swedish scientist, sails through the North-East passage and along the northern coast of Russia.
1903–1906	Roald Amundsen, a Norwegian explorer, sails through the North-West passage to reach the Arctic.

Key events in Ancient Britain

c. **100 000** B.C. ┼── The Old Stone Age — people were nomadic.

10 000 B.C. ┼── The Middle Stone Age — people were hunters and cave-dwellers.

6000 B.C. ┼── The New Stone Age — corn was grown for food; tools were made of flint.

2000 B.C. ┼── The Bronze Age.

1800 B.C. ┼── Stonehenge was started around this time.

1200 B.C. ┼── The arrival of the Celts.

750 B.C. ┼── Celtic settlements and farming.

400 B.C. ┼── Tribal wars. Trade in goods with Mediterranean countries.

54 B.C. ┼── Caesar's first expedition.

0 ┼── Roman civilisation expands and they colonise south-eastern Britain.

The birth of Christ in Asia

Earliest times – how do we know?

Radiocarbon dating

Counting annual growth rings

Archaeology – digging up remains, e.g. of bones, tools, pottery

Aerial photography

More about dates

Write down any one year from each century.

3rd century A.D.

1st century A.D.

12th century A.D.

4th century B.C.

6th century B.C.

19th century A.D.

Write down the century in which each date belongs.

A.D. 1736

421 B.C.

A.D. 306

A.D. 1992

3 B.C.

A.D. 1100

Focus on inventions

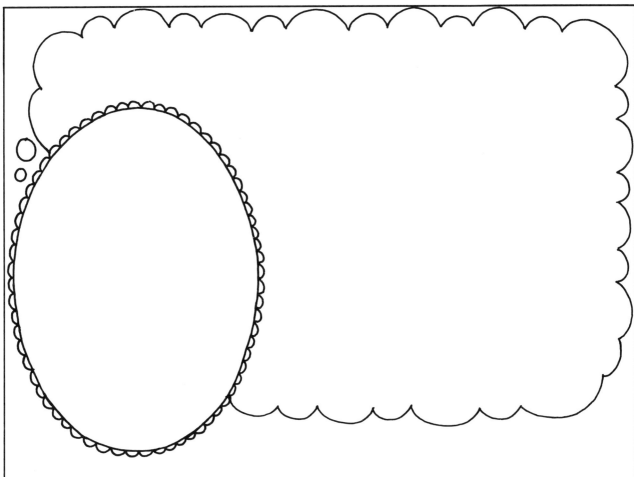

What is the invention? _____

Who invented it? When? _____

Did anything like it exist before? _____

Advantages	**Disadvantages**

Time sequence

Looking at objects

WHAT?

What is it made of?
What colour is it?
Are there signs of wear?
Does it smell?
Is it hand-made?
Is it valuable?

WHY?

Why was it made?
How was it used?
Why is it valued?
Why is it interesting?

WHO?

Who made it?
Who used it?
Who designed it?
Who values it?

WHEN?

When was it made?
How old is it?
Do we still have objects like it?
Has its use changed?

What they wore in Tudor times

cloak   doublet   hose   ruff   farthingale

wire headdress   wrist ruffles   breeches

The houses of history

NORMAN	PLANTAGENET	LANCASTER
YORK	TUDOR	STUART
HANOVER	SAXE-COBURG	WINDSOR

British monarchs 1066–1952

Norman kings

William the Conqueror	1066–87
William II	1087–1100
Henry I	1100–35
Stephen	1135–54

House of Plantagenets

Henry II	1154–89
Richard I	1189–99
John	1199–1216
Henry III	1216–72
Edward I	1272–1307
Edward II	1307–27
Edward III	1327–77
Richard II	1377–99

House of Lancaster

Henry IV	1399–1413
Henry V	1413–61
Henry VI	1422–61

House of York

Edward IV	1461–83
Edward V	1483
Richard III	1483–85

House of Tudor

Henry VII	1485–1509
Henry VIII	1509–47
Edward VI	1547–53
Mary I	1553–58
Elizabeth	1558–1603

House of Stuart

James I	1603–25
Charles I	1625–49

The Commonwealth

Between 1649 and 1660 the monarchy was abolished in Britain. The country became a republic* and was ruled by a Lord Protector and his council. The Lord Protectors were:

Oliver Cromwell	1649–59
Richard Cromwell	1659–60

House of Stuart (restored)

Charles II	1660–85
James II	1685–88
William III with	1688–1702
Mary II	1702–14

House of Hanover

George I	1714–27
George II	1727–60
George III	1760–1820
George IV	1820–30
William IV	1830–37

House of Saxe-Coburg-Gotha

(This was the family name of Queen Victoria's German husband, Prince Albert. It remained the name of the royal family until 1917 when it was changed to Windsor).

Victoria	1837–1901
Edward VII	1901–10

House of Windsor

George V	1910–36
Edward VIII	1936
George VI	1936–52
Elizabeth	1952–

Name: _____

Legacies

Art	Architecture	Music
Literature	Inventions	Discoveries
Famous Lives	International Links	Objects/Artefacts

Name: _____

A famous life

Name _____ Date of Birth _____

Date of Death _____ Historic House of Life _____

Personal Details: Family

Key Dates and Events

Main Legacy
and
Achievements

Sources of
Evidence

Historical vocabulary

Abdicate	
Baron	
Charter	
Democracy	
Depose	
Evidence	
Heresy	
Legacy	

Name: _____

Historical vocabulary

National	
Pagan	
Regent	
Religious/ Religious Freedom	
Sovereign	
Trade Union	
Treason	
Trial	

Summary sheet

Name of child _____

Date _____ Study unit _____	Date _____ Study unit _____
Level and comments	*Level and comments*
Level 2	Level 2
Level 3	Level 3
Level 4	Level 4
Level 5	Level 5
Date _____ Study unit _____	Date _____ Study unit _____
Level and comments	*Level and comments*
Level 2	Level 2
Level 3	Level 3
Level 4	Level 4
Level 5	Level 5

CLEANER COAL TECHNOLOGIES

Future plans for research and development,
technology transfer and export promotion

London: The Stationery Office

ISBN 0 11 515462 0

ENERGY PAPERS

This publication is number 67 in the series of Energy Papers published by the Department of Trade and Industry (DTI). This series is primarily intended to create a wider public understanding and discussion of energy matters, though some technical papers appear in it from time to time. The papers do not necessarily represent Government or Department policy.

Further information on the Cleaner Coal Technology Programme is available from:
Roshan Kamall
Location 1124
Department of Trade and Industry
1 Victoria Street
London SW1H 0ET
Tel: 0171 215 6261
Fax: 0171 828 7969
E-mail: roshan.kamal@hend.dti.gov.uk
Web: www.dti.gov.uk/ent/coal

Cover photograph: Low-NO_x Burner Flame
(Courtesy of Mitsui Babcock Energy)

Contents

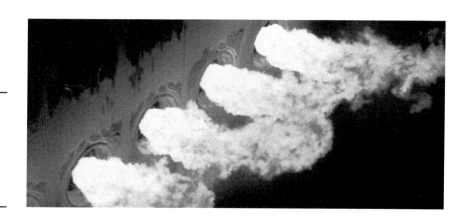

Foreword

There is a very large and growing world market for cleaner coal technologies, particularly for electricity generation. Recent International Energy Agency forecasts have indicated that some 38% of the world's electricity will still be generated from coal by 2020. Effectively this would mean a near doubling of coal use for electricity generation over the period 1995-2020. More efficient and environmentally-friendly cleaner coal technologies have therefore a major role to play in sustainable development worldwide. Widespread adoption of more efficient cleaner coal technologies, in both developed and developing countries, will help to reduce the projected growth in carbon dioxide and other emissions in the next century, and support the commitments made under the Kyoto Protocol in 1997.

UK industry is well placed to meet the challenge of developing more advanced cleaner coal technologies for electricity generation. The work of the Foresight Task Force, established by the Government to identify future UK research, development and demonstration needs in this area, is to be commended. The Task Force's summary report, which has been included in this Energy Paper, represents an excellent example of the type of collaboration the Government wishes to encourage between the science base and industry. The identification of clear technology targets for advanced power generation should enable industry and universities to work together to ensure that the UK maintains both its technical excellence in this area and its share of the growing world market.

Although UK companies have been successful in demonstrating cleaner coal technologies in world markets for a number of years, the recent emphasis in the UK on natural-gas-fired combined cycle gas turbine plant has resulted in the construction of no new coal-fired power stations since the completion of Drax in 1986. Consequently, in the UK, companies lack the facility to demonstrate advanced components, such as new boilers and turbines, to overseas customers. UK industry, however, has the capability to design and build advanced plant, for example supercritical technology, which could provide an additional focus for continuing research and development (R&D) and be a stepping stone for the planned development of even more advanced plant. As stated in the October 1998 White Paper, *Conclusions of the Review of Energy Sources for Power Generation*, the Government plans to review the case for supporting demonstration projects in about three years time.

The central theme of our new policy on cleaner coal technologies is to maintain strong support for R&D, and to make a financial contribution in partnership with industry and other funding agencies such as the European Commission's new Fifth Framework Programme. This policy will be implemented by a six-year programme strategy focused on contributing to the R&D recommendations of the Foresight Task Force. Department of Trade and Industry funding for the first three years will total some £12 million, which is forecast to generate projects worth at least £60 million. Additional funding may also be forthcoming, on a project by project basis, for cleaner-coal-related research supported by the Science Budget via the Engineering and Physical Sciences Research Council. As well as direct financial support to a portfolio of R&D projects, over the next few years the Government will also be initiating a series of focused trade missions and seminars in the key market areas to promote UK expertise and know-how. We also plan to produce a wide range of publications to help promote UK strengths in this important area.

Our programme will also be examining the opportunities offered by coal bed methane and underground coal gasification to contribute to the diversity and sustainability of the UK's future energy supply. A review of the specific research requirements of coal bed methane has already been initiated and we are exploring with the Coal Authority a number of options to take underground coal gasification forward. Here too, there is the exciting long-term prospect of widespread export applications of UK technologies and expertise.

John Battle, Energy and Industry Minister

1

cleaner coal technologies - "technologies designed to enhance both the efficiency and the environmental acceptability of coal extraction, preparation and use."

Introduction

1.1   The purpose of this document is to state the Government's policy on cleaner coal technology research, development and demonstration (R,D&D). It follows a detailed review of the achievements of the previous programme for cleaner coal research and development (R&D) over the past few years, the current status of the technologies and UK industry capability. The review also paid particular attention to the contribution the development of cleaner coal technologies could make to reducing the impact of climate change and the substantial export market that is likely to emerge during the next century particularly in Asia.

1.2   The October 1998 White Paper - Conclusions of the Review of Energy Sources for Power Generation (ref. 1) announced the decision by the Government to maintain a cleaner coal technology programme and to contribute to following up the recommendations of an industry-led Foresight Task Force. This Task Force was established by the Foresight Energy Panel to examine the long-term R,D&D priorities for cleaner coal power generation technologies. The Foresight programme is led by 16 panels set up to explore opportunities in different sectors of the economy. The panels published their first reports in 1995, following widespread consultation. The Energy panel identified nine priority themes, and set up industrially-led Task Forces covering two of the themes, one for Clean Coal Power Generation and one for Advanced Combined Cycle and Gas Turbine Technology, in order to develop Action Plans to implement the Foresight aims. The summary report of the Task Force covering cleaner coal power generation technology, which maps out the details of future UK technology requirements and the associated technical targets, is contained in Annex A.

1.3   This document sets out the rationale for a new DTI programme and describes the collaborative work planned with industry, universities and overseas organisations over the next six years. It also describes the technical targets established for the programme which will be used to monitor and evaluate the success of both projects and the programme as a whole.

1.4   Clean coal technologies may be defined as those technologies which improve the environmental acceptability of coal extraction, preparation and utilisation. They are most commonly associated with the utilisation of coal for power generation, and this is their main market. The technologies improve the environmental acceptability of power generation by reducing the proportions of sulphur and nitrogen oxides, and particulate emissions to the atmosphere. The higher efficiencies of converting coal into electricity, compared to conventional technologies used to generate much of the world's electricity, also mean that less carbon dioxide is produced with each unit of electricity. The pollutants of sulphur and nitrogen oxides (SO_2 and NO_x) cause acid rain and carbon dioxide is the most important greenhouse gas contributing to climate change. The technologies may be state-of-the-art, eg the integrated coal gasification combined cycle technology, or more advanced, supercritical forms of the conventional pulverised fuel technology used in the UK. The overall efficiency of such plant is more than 42% (lower heating value - LHV) compared to conventional coal plant currently used in the UK where efficiencies are around 38% with flue gas desulphurisation (FGD). Individual cleaner coal technology "components" such as FGD, low-NO_x burners and gas reburn technology, can be retrofitted to existing conventional plant to reduce emissions of SO_2 and NO_x. The addition of such abatement technology can make a useful contribution to extending the life of existing plant. The term "cleaner" is of course relative. Conventional pulverised fuel technology which is utilised in the UK could be called cleaner coal technology if compared with typical technology in developing countries such as China and India where plant efficiencies are nearly 10 percentage points less on average than at UK power plant. Annex B presents a concise guide to the main technologies and their current state of development. As indicated in the annex, the available technologies are not at the same stage of development nor are they likely to compete on environmental grounds with gas-fired combined cycle gas turbine (CCGT) plant - fuel chemistry puts cleaner coal at a disadvantage in carbon terms (ie the carbon intensity of the fuel) compared with gas plant of similar efficiency.

1.5   Coal-fired generation started in the UK in the 1890s using stoker-fired boilers. In the early days the efficiency of generation was quite low (5-7%) due mainly to low steam pressure and temperature. With the introduction of pulverised coal combustion in the 1920s and incremental increases in steam pressure and temperature over several decades due to developments in material technologies, the efficiency increased steadily and reached around 38% for subcritical plant with FGD fitted by the end of the 1980s. Further advances beyond 50% are likely to be achieved over the next decade as more advanced materials are developed for power station application. Figure 1 illustrates this gradual improvement in plant efficiency, which continues to this day with the development of supercritical pulverised fuel plant and gasification technology where efficiencies of around 45% are claimed. The curve shows data for the best plant.

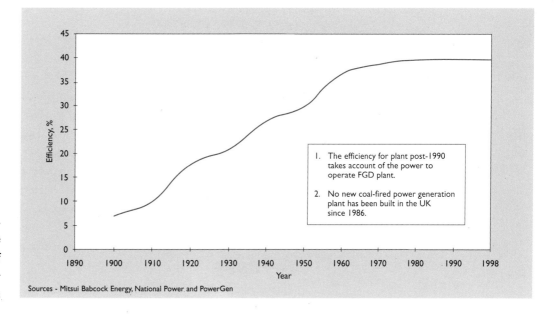

Figure 1. Improvements in the thermal efficiency of UK coal plant over the past 100 years

Sources - Mitsui Babcock Energy, National Power and PowerGen

1.6.   Figure 2 illustrates the emissions of carbon dioxide generated from coal against the thermal efficiency of electricity generation. The thermal efficiency varies with the system of power generation used. The solid part of the line represents the progress in current commercially available systems. The dotted line shows the progress expected with improvements in efficiency arising from future developments in materials and associated components. For comparison, the bottom line shows similar data for CCGT power generation plant.

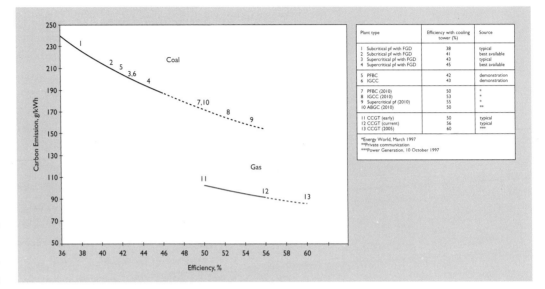

Figure 2. Carbon dioxide emissions from coal-fired plant compared with combined cycle gas turbine power plant

1.7   No cleaner coal technologies for new plant are currently economically competitive in the UK with existing conventional pulverised-coal-fired technology plant, whether or not these have been fitted with FGD equipment. The ability of new cleaner coal plant to compete with new gas plant depends on the availability and prices of gas and coal. These factors will vary from country to country since both gas and coal are costly to transport. They will also vary over time. In China and India, for example, the limited availability of natural gas, and substantial reserves of coal, mean that coal will play a major role in meeting electricity demand for the foreseeable future.

1.8   A number of the technologies, particularly the coal gasification technologies currently at the demonstration stage throughout the world, have technical issues to overcome before they can be considered to be commercially proven for large-scale electricity generation. The gasification technologies also have capital costs significantly higher than conventional coal plant and some three times the cost of CCGT plant at the present time. Versions of supercritical pulverised fuel plant fitted with FGD and NO_x reduction technology are perceived by generators as commercially proven. However, this technology also continues to develop in terms of increased steam temperature and pressure. The ultimate prospect of taking supercritical technology to temperatures of 700-750°C and efficiencies around 55% through deployment of new materials is thought to be achievable within ten years. The capital costs of recent supercritical coal plant are marginally higher than those of conventional coal plant but this gap is rapidly narrowing. The higher efficiency of such plant also means fuel costs are likely to be less over the lifetime of the plant which will be an important criterion for a utility selecting new power generation capacity.

1.9   There are a number of commercial-scale demonstration plant being supported which should resolve many of the technical issues over the next few years. This is particularly the case for the coal gasification technologies. However, it is most unlikely that the capital costs of such plant will be able to compete with gas for the foreseeable future. Where coal is the only real choice of fuel, or where some coal capacity is required for fuel diversity, such plant should be able to offer substantial reductions in acid emissions and carbon dioxide (some 20% or more in developing countries) when compared to existing coal plant. There also may be some limited opportunities which allow for the commercial application of cleaner coal technologies in the UK over the next few years. For example, Global Energy is proposing to build a 400MW$_e$ plant in Fife, Scotland, which would utilise coal gasification and waste-derived fuel to produce a synthetic gas which would be its main fuel; this would be burnt with natural gas to generate electricity. The proposal's application under section 36 of the Electricity Act 1989 is currently before the Secretary of State for Scotland. Such "hybrid" projects, if they proceed, may provide opportunities to extend the experience of different types of cleaner coal technology over the next few years.

1.10   A previous Coal R&D Programme was in operation from 1993 until 1998 and was described in Energy Paper 63 published in October 1994 (ref. 2). The main objective of this programme was to provide transitional support to complete the strategic R&D programme of British Coal following privatisation. This work has now been successfully completed and industry is taking forward the development of technologies covering the complete coal cycle from mining through to utilisation. A detailed set of technical and administrative targets were established for the programme described in Energy Paper 63. Annex C indicates the extent to which these detailed targets were met.

1.11   An evaluation in 1996 (ref. 3) found that the programme described in Energy Paper 63 had encouraged a significant level of collaborative R&D activity in the UK between industry, universities and overseas organisations that would not otherwise have taken place. However, despite the progress made, it identified the need for continuing Government involvement in the form of a new programme if the objectives for this sector were to be achieved and remaining market deficiencies addressed.

1.12   A review of the future UK R,D&D requirements was undertaken by the DTI to examine what further work it needed to support following completion of the programme described in Energy Paper 63 and the 1996 evaluation report. The results of the review, which was completed in 1998, have been incorporated into this Energy Paper. This review took account of the views of the advisory committee for the programme and the observations of the international panel of experts who undertook the evaluation exercise in 1996. A key input to the review process was the work undertaken during 1998 on cleaner coal power generation by an industry-led Task Force established by the Foresight Energy Panel (see paragraphs 2.5-2.8 and Annex A) as part of the Office of Science and Technology's Foresight programme.

Coal bed methane and underground coal gasification

1.13   The review process also examined the potential of coal bed methane (CBM) and underground coal gasification in the UK. During the consultation exercise for the Government's review of energy sources for power generation, a number of consultees suggested that CBM and underground coal gasification would provide an alternative way to obtain the energy from coal without mining. In the October 1998 White Paper which set out the Government's conclusions on the review, it agreed that in the longer-term these technologies might provide some form of access to the large-scale UK coal resources inaccessible by conventional mining - including substantial resources under the North Sea. However, these technologies are a long way from being considered an alternative to conventional mining with a substantial R&D effort required to enable the resource to be exploited in the longer-term.

1.14   In respect of CBM, the review identified three potential areas of interest to the UK:

● the development of its indigenous CBM reserves to contribute to the diversity and sustainability of the UK's future energy supply;

● the opportunity for UK companies to exploit their experience overseas;

● the contribution CBM technology may make to increasing the life of North Sea gas reserves.

1.15   If CBM technology can be made to work in the UK as in the US, then the technology should be exportable worldwide with key geographical areas of interest including China, India and Eastern Europe. Both China and India have coal reserves which considerably exceed their oil and natural gas reserves. They both have increasing primary energy requirements, as the standard of living of their populations rises. CBM could therefore be a useful, and potentially clean, source of energy.

1.16   The successful application of CBM technology on the UK mainland could also have an important spin-off in extending the life of the North Sea natural gas fields. For CBM technology to be economic on the UK mainland, more innovative drilling and production methods will need to be developed which may have offshore application. Although the big offshore gas fields are not suited to CBM technology, it could have an important niche market in many of the smaller fields. Further details on the potential of CBM and the way forward identified by the review are presented in Annex D.

1.17   A considerable amount of work has already been undertaken on developing underground coal gasification technology and the DTI has been supporting a major field trial of the technology for a number of years in Spain. This is a joint Spanish, Belgian and UK project with substantial financial support from the European Commission's Framework Programme. This field trial has now been completed and has successfully demonstrated that it is possible to gasify European coals at depths in excess of 500 metres and to produce good quality gas - comparable to that obtained from coal gasification plant used for electricity generation. Further details of the potential of underground coal gasification and the way forward identified by the review are presented in Annex E.

The future market - world and UK

1.18   The markets for cleaner coal technologies are driven by two factors: increasing demand for electricity and increasing environmental constraints. Despite the recent Asian economic crisis which has had a major impact on the development of new power stations, coal use worldwide for electricity generation is forecast by the International Energy Agency (IEA) to still grow significantly over the next 20 years, particularly in China and many developing countries (IEA World Energy Outlook, ref. 4, and Figures 3, 4, and 5). The IEA forecasts indicate that solid fuel (mainly coal but includes peat, combustible renewables and waste) retains a strong position in power generation. It is the favoured fuel where gas is unavailable or expensive (like China and India), or in locations close to low-cost coal production (parts of North America, Australia and South Africa). Figure 5 in particular, emphasises the substantial increase in China's dependence on coal to meet its future electricity requirements.

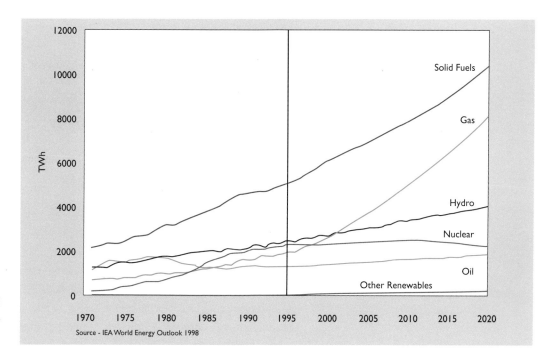

Figure 3. World electricity generation by fuel

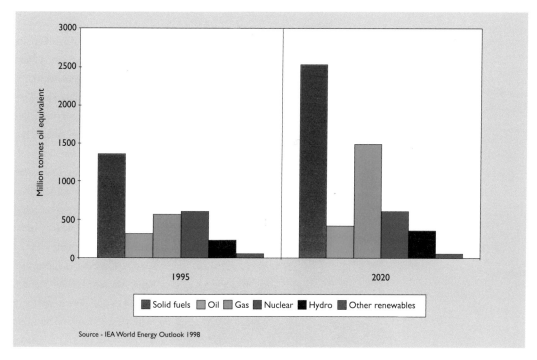

Figure 4. World power generation inputs by fuel – 1995 and 2020

1.19   This growing market represents one of the biggest export opportunities for UK plant and equipment companies worth up to £300 billion over the next decade or so - with much more beyond. The UK's share of this market, if it can retain its current proportion of the world power equipment market, could be some £30 billion over the next ten years or so. The UK power equipment industry is an important sector of the economy employing some 165,000 people with a £13.3 billion turnover in 1997 (ref. 5). As such, securing an appropriate share of the future world market for the technologies will have long-term benefit for the industry. Several countries have already recognised the importance of developing and applying cleaner coal technologies and the UK is facing considerable competition in this field.

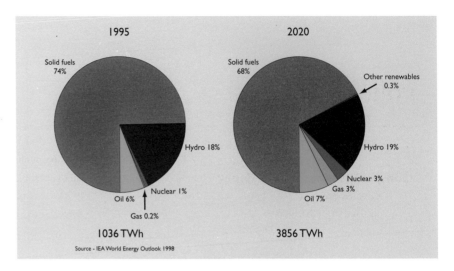

Figure 5. Electricity generation in China

1.20   The market is expected to be split between conventional coal-fired plant and more advanced supercritical plant as well as some limited fluidised bed combustion and gasification plant.   Studies by the IEA and others suggest that conventional and supercritical plant will predominate taking some 80% of the market.   Even conventional coal-fired power plant with efficiencies typical of current UK plant would have a major impact on reducing carbon dioxide emissions in developing countries such as China.

1.21   There are proposals to build nearly $2GW_e$ of cleaner coal technology plant in the UK at the present time.   Most of these proposals would utilise technology already demonstrated at commercial scale elsewhere in the world.   Current UK coal capacity totals some $30GW_e$ and there could be opportunities for new plant to be built in consequence of increased demand or retirement of other generating plant (of whatever kind).   What proportion of any new plant is advanced cleaner coal technology will depend on a number of factors, not least the competitiveness and reliability of the technologies compared to other generation technologies together with their ability to meet future emission regulations. The UK market for the short to medium term offers a number of opportunities

A view of PowerGen's Ratcliffe Power Station in the UK, which uses both NO_x (low-NO_x burners) and SO_2 (wet scrubbing FGD process) abatement equipment

for retrofit of more advanced pollution control equipment and associated components, eg FGD, gas reburn technology and other low NO_x equipment.   The recent announcement by Eastern Generation Ltd to invest in new FGD equipment at West Burton Power Station highlights the potential for retrofit opportunities for UK industry over the next few years.

1.22   UK strengths in clean coal technology were identified by the Foresight Task Force to be in advanced pf, the air blown gasification cycle (ABGC), and the (oxygen blown) integrated gasification combined cycle (IGCC). Further details of UK strengths, and UK and world markets for clean coal technologies, are presented in the summary report from the Foresight Task Force at Annex A.

2

Policy Framework

The Government's Competitiveness White Paper - Our Competitive Future: Building the Knowledge-Driven Economy

2.1   The White Paper (ref. 6), published in December 1998 sets out a modern industrial policy to help British business meet the challenge of the knowledge-driven economy. The White Paper challenges British business to close the performance gap with its competitors, in terms of both productivity and its ability to produce innovative new products and create high-value services; and it outlines the catalytic role Government has to play. The Government's first job is to ensure a stable macro-economic environment but it must also promote open, competitive markets, invest to strengthen underlying economic capabilities such as science and entrepreneurship and facilitate creative collaborations between companies.

2.2   The White Paper highlights the fact that, in today's global economy, technology can migrate quickly and goods can be made in low-cost countries and shipped to developed markets. British business must compete by exploiting capabilities which competitors cannot easily match or imitate - knowledge, skills and creativity which can help create high-productivity business processes and high-value goods and services. In the power sector, the major components of conventional power plant are increasingly being supplied by the home market in developing countries such as China and India rather than by overseas companies. Such markets will only remain open to UK industry if it can continue to supply more advanced components which offer improvements in efficiency, environmental performance and innovation etc.

Air pollution around a steel plant in China

The Government's White Paper - Conclusions of the Review of Energy Sources for Power Generation

2.3   The White Paper (ref. 1) set out the detail of the Government's central energy policy objective to ensure secure, diverse and sustainable supplies of energy at competitive prices. This objective takes in the Government's concern for the environment, health and safety and a fair deal for all consumers, as well as its commitment to all aspects of sustainable development. The White Paper emphasised the considerable importance of security of energy supply to both industry and consumers. Diversity is closely linked to security of supply; the Paper highlighted the need for an acceptable level of diversity and that coal remains important as a main contributor to the diversity and flexibility of UK electricity production into the foreseeable future. Cleaner coal technologies have an important role to play in the sustainability of energy worldwide, not just in the UK. The White Paper also signposted the Government's policy for cleaner coal set out in detail in this Energy Paper and accepted the recommendations of the Foresight Task Force that further work on cleaner coal power generation technologies was a priority task - both because of its substantial export potential and because it could provide a major element of a programme to contain the growth in carbon dioxide worldwide and reduce emissions.

2.4   In the White Paper the Government emphasised that a new programme, by contributing to meeting the Foresight targets, would:

- enable the UK to maintain and develop its know-how and expertise in the technologies, so helping UK manufacturing industry to obtain a significant share of the world market;

- act as a focus for collaboration between industry, universities and overseas organisations, so strengthening the link between industry and the science base;

- enable the DTI to contribute to a global strategy to contain the growth of carbon dioxide in developing countries in collaboration with the IEA.

Foresight and rationale for Government support for R&D

2.5   A key element of the Government's science policy is the Foresight programme which was first announced in the 1993 White Paper, Realising our Potential (ref. 7). Its aim is to create a sustainable competitive advantage and enhance the quality of life, by bringing together business, the science base and Government to identify and respond to emerging opportunities in markets and technologies.

2.6   To date (changes due to take effect in April were announced last December, ref. 8) Foresight has operated through 16 panels set up to explore opportunities in different sectors of the economy. The panels' first reports were published in 1995 following widespread consultation and aimed to identify:

- the likely social, economic and market trends that will affect the UK in the medium to long-term

- the developments required in science, engineering and technology to best address future needs

- the implications for policy and infrastructure and for business investment strategies.

2.7   The Foresight Energy Panel identified cleaner coal power generation technology as an area likely to make a major contribution to UK wealth creation well into the 21st century. Cleaner coal technology is seen as offering substantial future export opportunities for manufacturers of both power plant and component suppliers to that industry, resulting from expected growth in coal use by developing countries. Future benefit to UK manufacturers from these opportunities is however dependent on undertaking further significant R&D, the returns from which are uncertain and will only be enjoyed in some years time.

2.8   Following cleaner coal technology being identified as a priority sector under Foresight, a Task Force was established by the Foresight Energy Panel to develop an action plan to take forward the initiative. This action plan recommended supporting R&D to meet a specific set of technology targets for advanced clean coal plant covering capital and through-life costs, efficiency, emissions, plant reliability and maintainability, and fuel flexibility. The summary report from the industry-led Task Force at Annex A describes the research priorities to achieve these technology targets and includes an analysis of UK strengths and markets for the technologies. DTI contributed around half of the cost of the Task Force work, industry providing the remainder.

2.9   There is a general consensus worldwide that cleaner coal technologies will not become widespread on a commercial scale until 2010 at the earliest in OECD countries, with perhaps a few subsidised plant in developing countries at that time. Conventional plant of the type now in operation in the UK, perhaps with retrofitting of clean-up technology, is expected to be the commercial plant of choice for developing countries over most of the period up to 2010. R&D into cleaner coal technology does not therefore offer companies any real prospect of returns from much of their investment in the short to medium term.

2.10   The effect of the programme should be to stimulate additional R&D expenditure by companies in this sector greatly exceeding in value the amount of Government support provided. Government involvement will also assist the UK to benefit from international research funding aimed at this sector through the European Union and from the collaborative activities initiated under the auspices of the IEA. The evaluation of the previous programme found that "seed corn" funding by DTI had enabled 80% of the cost of the programme to be provided by industry and other funding agencies. The evaluators considered it "most unlikely that any other organisation public or private could have provided the necessary focus for this level of gearing to be achieved".

2.11   Government involvement by initiating a new Cleaner Coal Technology Programme should, by contributing some financial support to projects and encouraging collaboration, accelerate development work on cleaner coal technology which would otherwise be on a smaller scale and much slower in being progressed. This would otherwise be to the disadvantage of UK exporters once the overseas market for these technologies takes off. The collaborative function of the programme is particularly important in combining the efforts of industry and universities to progress UK technology in this sector and enabling access to overseas programmes via bilateral and multilateral collaborations initiated by Government. The programme would also facilitate collaborative research activities with developing countries and further enhance the building of long-term relationships which underpin future export opportunities.

2.12   A further significant element of the rationale for this programme is the contribution that cleaner coal technology would make to achieving international environmental goals by technology transfer to major coal-using developing countries. This element is one of a number of positive contributions by the Government as part of its overall climate change policy. The new programme described later in this document outlines a number of initiatives the DTI has already started and has planned for this important area.

Government policy with respect to demonstration projects

2.13   A final, but nonetheless important, rationale for maintaining support for an R&D programme is to identify the extent to which all the extensive coal resources of the UK can be used as a source of energy in the future. Both coal bed methane and underground coal gasification technology offer some promise to contribute to future energy supply in the longer-term - if they can be successfully developed commercially on a large scale.

2.14   The policy of successive Governments has been not to grant substantial financial support towards cleaner coal demonstration projects where the R&D stage of technology development has been successfully completed at pilot plant stage. Public sector funding focuses its contribution on the high risk, strategic R&D end of cleaner coal technology development. This was emphasised in Energy Paper 63, published in October 1994, with a commitment to keep the situation under review in light of uncertainties about the impact of environmental regulations and other market developments.

2.15   The term "demonstration" carries the implication that a particular technology would need to be demonstrated at a commercial scale to give confidence to prospective purchasers that the technology can deliver appropriate guarantees covering reliability, maintainability, efficiency, load factor etc. Many, if not most, of the projects seeking Government support over the past few years have in fact already been demonstrated successfully at commercial scale elsewhere in the world. However, the higher capital costs compared to conventional coal plant, and especially CCGT, ruled out their selection unless a subsidy is available in some form, or innovative mechanisms can be found to make the projects commercial.

2.16   As explained in the 1998 White Paper on the Conclusions of the Review of Energy Sources for Power Generation, the position in respect to the UK electricity generation industry is different from a number of overseas countries because there is currently a surplus of existing coal-fired capacity which uses moderately efficient $500MW_e$ generating units. This opens the UK industry to an approach of incremental improvements to existing plant, together with the strategic installation of FGD on the most heavily used stations rather than investment in new coal plant. Although the environmental benefits from such an approach are not as good as those obtainable from currently available cleaner coal plant, the difference is not sufficiently decisive as yet to justify the very large differences in costs between the two approaches.

2.17   In light of these considerations the DTI did not feel that funding the construction of currently available cleaner coal plant, whether by way of a direct grant or some kind of levy would constitute value for money at present. However, this position could change if more advanced technologies emerge from the Foresight work which offer decisive advantage in UK circumstances that current commercially-available technology lacks. The Foresight summary report identified a case for demonstration from around 2005 and Government will re-examine the position in about three years time as part of a planned review and evaluation of progress of the new R&D programme.

International collaboration

2.18   The UK is not alone in recognising the importance of cleaner coal technologies both in terms of the contribution the widespread use of more efficient technologies would make to the environment and to reducing the impact of climate change, and of the significant world export market for the foreseeable future - well into the 21st century. A key focus of international collaborative activity in this area is the IEA.

2.19   The DTI has played a leading role in the IEA for a number of years by initiating and establishing a number of important R&D and technology transfer collaborations. The key areas where IEA work on cleaner coal technology has taken place over the past few years and is expected to continue for the foreseeable future with strong support from DTI are highlighted in Table 1.

Table 1 - Key areas of IEA activity where work on cleaner coal technology is undertaken

IEA Working Party on Fossil Fuels

The DTI provides the chair of this Working Party which is responsible for advising the IEA on fossil fuel technology-related policies, priorities, programmes and strategies that address the long-term energy security and environmental protection interests of Member countries. Under the auspices of the Working Party, the UK has initiated a number of collaborative projects, and published reports on the status of cleaner coal technologies and market information. It has also initiated a number of activities to help developing countries become more informed about cleaner coal technologies.

In addition the Working Party oversees all the IEA fossil fuel collaborative R&D agreements and undertakes regular reviews and evaluations of programmes.

Further information can be found on the internet: http://www.iea.org

IEA Coal Research – The Clean Coal Centre

This information centre is based in the UK and provides impartial and objective information and assessment on all aspects of coal-related technologies and economics. The research reports are publicly available to anyone in the UK. The service is governed by representatives of 13 Member countries and the European Commission. UK industry plays an active part in contributing to the work programme of the Centre as well as making a significant financial contribution together with the DTI.

Further information can be found on the internet: http://www.iea-coal.org.uk

IEA Greenhouse Gas R&D Programme

The Operating Agent for this Agreement is also based in the UK. It was established by the UK and aims to:

- identify and evaluate technologies for reducing emissions of greenhouse gases arising from use of fossil fuels;
- disseminate the results of these studies;
- identify targets for R,D&D and promote the appropriate work.

Its main activities concern methods of reducing greenhouse gas emissions, particularly carbon dioxide from power generation. Other sources of greenhouse gases are also being examined, including methods of reducing methane emissions.

Further information can be found on the internet: http://www.ieagreen.org.uk

2.20   Support for cleaner coal R,D&D has been available for a number of years from the European Commission. For example, some funding is likely to be available from the European Commission for UK participation alongside other Member States in EU based demonstration projects via the European Commission's Fifth Framework Programme for R,D&D. A number of UK companies were successful in obtaining grant aid under the Fourth Framework Programme.   These included ScottishPower who successfully demonstrated gas reburn technology at their Longannet Power Station, Scotland.

2.21   The first call for proposals under the Fifth Framework Programme will be made this year. A key objective of the new DTI Cleaner Coal Programme will be to assist UK companies in putting forward proposals for grant aid from the Commission from the Framework Programme. The DTI and the Foresight Task Force have kept the Commission fully informed of the recommendations arising from the Foresight work on cleaner coal technology and these are expected to be reflected in the Commission's own priorities for R,D&D for the Framework Programme. The Commission also supports a separate, general Energy Framework Programme which is partially concerned with the promotion of clean coal technology for its export potential.

2.22   Coal R&D has also been supported for many years by the European Coal and Steel Community (ECSC) Programme. This programme has supported research on both mining-related topics and coal utilisation for power and industrial uses. UK industry and universities have received substantial support for a wide range of cleaner coal R&D projects over the past few years from this programme.

2.23   The ECSC Treaty will expire on 23 July 2002. At that date there is expected to be a sizeable reserve representing levies which the Commission has imposed on the production of coal and steel in accordance with Article 49 of the ECSC Treaty. At the Amsterdam summit in 1997 the Commission was invited to make proposals to "use the revenues of outstanding reserves for a research fund for sectors related to the coal and steel industry". The precise balance of research activities in a future programme post 2002 has yet to be finalised by the Commission. The allocation of funds between the coal and steel sectors also remains to be decided. Some 30 million Euros are expected to be available annually from the ECSC programme post 2002 for coal- and steel-related research. The Government will be pressing that the ECSC research budget should be increasingly focused on coal utilisation R&D rather than on coal production research in support of the heavily subsidised mines of much of Europe. Exceptions to this would be where research can lead to improvements in safety, enhance mine productivity of economic mines, and assist the coal mining equipment industry in developing components and know-how for overseas applications.

2.24   A number of bilateral collaborative agreements have also been initiated which provide further opportunities for universities and industry to collaborate with overseas partners. The Memorandum of Understanding (MOU) on Energy R&D between the DTI and the United States Department of Energy has provided some valuable exchanges of information and R&D collaboration. Two UK companies, British Gas and British Steel, have also been successful in having their technologies included in the US Clean Coal Demonstration Programme. A recently signed MOU on R&D collaboration with China also offers further potential to develop an important portfolio of research projects between Chinese research organisations and UK industry and universities. Three new R&D collaborative projects with China are now under way with a value of nearly £400,000 involving four UK companies and three universities.

3

Cleaner Coal Technologies
Policy and Programme Strategy

Policy 3.1 Government policy is to encourage the development of cleaner coal technologies for application in both home and overseas markets and therefore contribute to:

- reducing the global environmental impact of coal use for both power and industrial applications;

- enhancing UK manufacturing industry's competitiveness;

- increasing the potential to economically exploit UK coal resources by innovative methods.

3.2 This policy will be implemented by establishing a six year collaborative programme of activities linking R&D with technology transfer and export promotion activities. The new programme will act as a catalyst for this collaboration to take place and establish partnership activities with other organisations (UK and overseas-based) with an interest in the development of the technologies, eg the Coal Authority, the Engineering and Physical Sciences Research Council (EPSRC), the British Coal Utilisation Research Association (BCURA), the IEA, the European Commission, the US Department of Energy and science and technology institutions in developing countries.

3.3 The R&D activities will focus on establishing a portfolio of projects to contribute to meeting the Foresight technology targets on advanced power generation. R&D will also be supported to develop the UK's coal bed methane and underground coal gasification resource. Concise summaries of these technologies and the proposed way forward are set out in Annexes D and E.

3.4 A number of partnership activities have already been initiated for the new programme and include:

- working with the Coal Authority to identify options and R&D needs for developing the potential of coal bed methane and underground coal gasification technology for UK application;

- establishing a Memorandum of Understanding with China to undertake collaborative R&D and promote cleaner coal technology;

- establishing a new collaborative agreement with BCURA to jointly support projects aimed at contributing to the Foresight recommendations together with university-based research on coal bed methane and underground coal gasification;

- establishing a new collaborative agreement with EPSRC to jointly support fundamental coal science and technology issues identified by the Foresight exercise;

- initiating under the auspices of the IEA a major project to identify cost-effective ways of improving the efficiency and environmental performance of existing Chinese coal power plant;

- initiating under the auspices of the IEA a range of publications and seminars to promote cleaner coal technology and help reduce the non-technical market barriers to their development;

- exploring with the US Department of Energy areas for future collaboration under the US/UK Memorandum of Understanding on Energy R&D;

- helping to initiate and establish a major R&D collaboration on advanced supercritical technology under the auspices of the European Commission's Framework Programme;

- participating in a major international project based in Canada to investigate the potential for using carbon dioxide sequestration technology in exploiting coal bed methane reserves in partnership with US and Canadian Government research organisations and industry.

3.5   A number of further international collaborative projects are expected to be initiated over the next six years. Details of all these projects will be published in project profiles and summary reports by the DTI. Information will also be available on the internet through the DTI home page (http:// www.dti.gov.uk).

Programme strategy   3.6   The broad aim of the new programme is therefore:

"To provide a catalyst for UK industry to develop cleaner coal technologies and obtain an appropriate share of the growing world market for the technologies".

This "catalyst role" will essentially be provided by the new DTI programme acting as a focus to encourage collaboration between UK industry and universities to develop new technologies and expertise. This focus will be provided in a number of ways. Firstly, DTI will be making a financial contribution to a portfolio of projects contracted with industry and universities. A number of these projects are expected to be jointly funded projects with EPSRC with support from the Science Budget. Over the first three years of the programme, the DTI contribution of some £12 million is expected to generate projects valued at some £60 million with support from both Government, industry and the European Commission's Fifth Framework Programme. This will make an important contribution to kick-starting the £176 million, 5 year programme, proposed by the Foresight Task Force in their summary report (see Annex A). Secondly, it will be supporting a wide range of seminars, workshops and trade missions to promote UK technology and foster international collaboration. Within the total DTI contribution, expenditure on these export promotion and technology transfer activities is expected to total some £500,000 per annum over the next few years. These will be undertaken by the DTI's Energy Technology Directorate in partnership with the Export Directorates in the

DTI. A number of export promotion activities have already taken place under the auspices of the DTI Power Sector Working Group. Details of these technology transfer and export promotion activities are presented in Annex F. Thirdly, the DTI will provide assistance to industry in seeking grant aid from the European Commission's Fifth Framework Programme for R&D and demonstration projects. The programme will also give some support to examining the extent to which the non-technical barriers to getting UK-based cleaner coal technology power projects off the ground over the next few years can be overcome. This issue will be explored further with the trade associations for both the coal industry and the power manufacturing industry.

Programme objectives

3.7　　The objectives that will be used to meet the aim of the programme are:

- to assist industry in meeting the technology targets for advanced power generation set out in the Foresight summary report (70%);

- to encourage the development of an internationally competitive cleaner coal component industry and promote UK expertise and know-how in the main export markets (10%);

- to encourage fundamental coal science research in support of the Foresight recommendations in collaboration with EPSRC and BCURA (5%);

- to examine, in partnership with the Coal Authority and industry, the potential for developing the UK coal bed methane resource and underground coal gasification technology (15%).

(The approximate percentage of the annual budget that is expected to be assigned to each objective is presented in brackets.)

Programme performance targets

3.8　　The main technical performance targets are set out in Annex A for the Foresight work and Annexes D and E for the coal bed methane and underground coal gasification R&D activities, and these are summarised in Table 2. A detailed set of administrative and technical targets will also be set for the programme on an annual basis and published in an annual report. The report will also be made available on the DTI home page together with details of progress in meeting these targets. The extent to which the programme has contributed to assisting industry meet the main technical targets will be evaluated at two stages - after three years, and at the end of the programme using external evaluators. Details of the monitoring and evaluation activities for the new programme are presented in Annex G.

Advisory Committee on Cleaner Coal Technology

3.9　　A new advisory committee is being established to oversee the new programme and its terms of reference are presented in Annex H. The new committee will have a membership drawn from equipment manufacturers, generating companies and universities. Representation will also be sought from the coal industry and mining equipment manufacturing trade associations since an important role of the committee will be to advise on technology transfer and export promotion issues associated with the whole of the coal cycle. A key role of this committee will be peer review of R&D project proposals to ensure they offer promise of contributing to meeting the technology targets established by Foresight.

Table 2 - Main technology targets for the programme	**A. Technology targets for advanced power generation R&D projects:**	Capital and through-life costs that compete effectively with those for sub-critical pulverised fuel plant incorporating low-NO_x burners and FGD
		Plant thermal efficiency levels to exceed 50% (based on the lower heating value of the fuel)
		Emission levels equal to or better than those proposed for developed countries
		Plant reliability, availability, maintainability and operability (RAMO) which exceeds current best practice
		Plant that is capable of accepting a wide range of fuels
	B. Technology targets for coal bed methane (CBM) activities of the programme:	Devise better mechanical methods of enhancing the permeability of UK coals
		Obtain reliable estimates of the costs of CBM extraction and, in particular, identify significant cost components
		Examine and cost two options for enhancing CBM release. Examples include carbon dioxide and nitrogen injection
		Identify the other key CBM release parameters
		Determine the current UK reserves of CBM and consider ways that these could be increased
		Achieve commercial CBM extraction in at least one coalfield area, preferably in more than one location in that area
		Identify the "break even" conditions which would have to be achieved if CBM is to compete with North Sea gas.
	C. Technology targets for underground coal gasification (UCG) activities of the programme:	Improve the accuracy of in-seam drilling to achieve a 400m run in a 2m seam, on a consistent basis
		Examine the implications of burning the gas produced in the Spanish UCG trial in a gas turbine
		Produce an estimate of the landward reserves of coal which could be technically suitable for UCG; in the first instance this could be coal seams at least 2m thick and at a depth not exceeding 1200m
		Identify a site for a semi-commercial trial of UCG; this would require a block of coal about 600m by 600m and with a seam thickness of at least 2m
		Identify the parameters that UCG would have to meet if it were to be competitive with current North Sea production costs
		Carry out a pre-feasibility study for the exploitation of UCG offshore in the southern North Sea

Expenditure   3.10   Planned expenditure by the DTI over the next three years on cleaner coal technology R&D is £12 million with expenditure for the subsequent three years determined by the next Comprehensive Spending Review exercise. Figure 6 illustrates the expected breakdown of expenditure over the next few years. However, this expenditure only represents the DTI's contribution to a much larger UK-based R&D activity which is expected to be initiated because of the focus provided by the programme. If the gearing of 4:1 of the past programme is maintained, R&D activity well in excess of £60 million would be generated over the next three years with more beyond. The collaborative activities highlighted above will also give industry and universities access to the results of substantial overseas programmes.

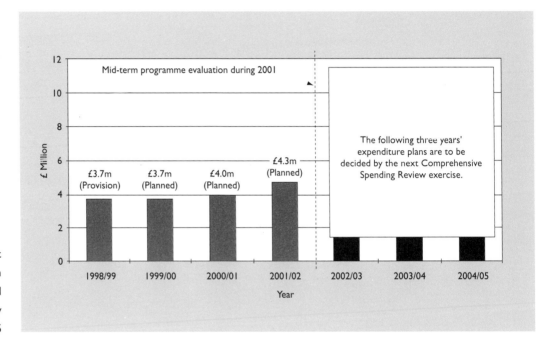

Figure 6. Net expenditure on cleaner coal technology 1998-2005

Low-NO$_x$
Burner Flame

Courtesy of Mitsui Babcock Energy

Annex A

Summary Report of Foresight

Objective

A costed Research, Development and Demonstration (R,D&D) programme, sufficient to ensure that the UK holds and extends its market position in the field of cleaner coal power plant technology, has been prepared by a group drawn from UK industry. The programme defines the necessary R,D&D work required to meet the technology targets and timescales identified by the Cleaner Coal Technology Task Force of the Foresight Energy Panel. Financial assistance for this work has been given by the DTI through its Cleaner Coal Technology Programme and the EPSRC.

Background To Foresight

The UK's Foresight programme was first announced in 1993 in the White Paper, Realising our Potential (ref. 7). Its aims are to create sustainable competitive advantage and enhance the quality of life, by bringing together business, the science base and Government, to identify and respond to emerging opportunities in markets and technologies.

The Foresight programme is led by 16 panels set up to explore opportunities in different sectors of the economy. The panels published their first reports in 1995, following widespread consultation. The Energy panel identified nine priority themes, and set up industrially-led Task Forces covering two of the themes, both focused on power generation, one for Cleaner Coal Technology and one for Advanced Combined Cycle and Gas Turbine Technology, in order to develop Action Plans to implement the Foresight Aims. This report describes the development of an R,D&D programme for cleaner coal technology, a key component of the Action Plan. A parallel study initiated by the Advanced Combined Cycle and Gas Turbine Technology Task Force is working on the production of an R,D&D programme for combined cycle and gas turbine technology with the objective of establishing an integrated advanced power generation programme embracing both technological areas.

The Cleaner Coal Technology Task Force

In order to develop an Action Plan to hold and extend the UK's strong market position in cleaner coal technology, the Task Force carried out the following:

a) identified the future worldwide market for new coal power plant to be between 430 and 560GW$_e$ over the next 15 years, with 70% being in Asia and around 80% of the overall plant required being conventional and advanced pulverised fuel (pf); the remainder would be fluidised bed and coal gasification plant with gas turbine/steam turbine combined cycles. [Note: in this report, advanced pf is used synonymously with pf plant employing supercritical or ultrasupercritical steam conditions.]

b) identified the strengths of the UK industry to be in advanced pf, the air blown gasification cycle (ABGC), and the (oxygen blown) integrated gasification combined cycle (IGCC).

c) defined the following technology targets:

- capital and through-life costs that compete effectively with those for sub-critical pf plant incorporating low-NO_x burners and flue gas desulphurisation (FGD);

- Plant thermal efficiency levels to exceed 50% (based on the lower calorific value of the fuel);

- emission levels equal to or better than those proposed for developed countries;

- plant reliability, availability, maintainability and operability (RAMO) which exceeds current best practice;

- plant that is capable of accepting a wide range of fuels.

d) identified the key components and the underpinning science and technologies required to achieve the technology targets.

e) set the following timescales:

- plant design and component demonstration by 2005;

- component and system demonstration between 2005 and 2010;

- commercially competitive plant between 2010 and 2020.

However the programme would also be expected to recognise the need for R,D&D to meet intermediate targets over shorter timescales, taking into account the fact that conventional pf plant would continue to have a major market share, and that many of the technology developments carried out for advanced pf, ABGC and IGCC will have application to conventional pf. [Note: a broad technical description of each of these technologies is given in Annex C.]

The importance of coal as a fuel

Coal is a major fuel in the generation of electricity worldwide. In spite of the increase in the use of natural gas for power generation, coal production rose 55% between 1973 and 1992, and is expected to rise by a further 40% between 1993 and 2010 (ref. 9). In addition, identified reserves of coal far exceed those of oil and natural gas, and are predicted to last for up to 100 years, even taking into account the projected increase in the rate of production.

Emissions

Conventional combustion of coal releases significant quantities of carbon dioxide (CO_2), and can potentially release sulphur dioxide (SO_2), oxides of nitrogen (NO_x) and particulates into the atmosphere. CO_2 adds to the greenhouse gases in the atmosphere, and the other gases combine with water to produce acid rain, ozone layer depletion and photochemical smog. Increased coal use therefore will cause major damage to the environment, unless methods are used to eliminate these problems. The challenge to the power plant industry is to produce "cleaner coal" plant for the generation of electricity, whilst maintaining its cost competitiveness against plant using other fuels.

Cleaner coal power plant

All cleaner coal plant have the same objectives, namely to improve efficiency of energy conversion whilst reducing costs and emissions to acceptable levels.

Of the three power plant types, advanced pf, ABGC and IGCC, identified by the Task Force, ABGC and IGCC are seen as new technologies. However, IGCC has been demonstrated at a commercial scale whereas ABGC is only at the individual component demonstration stage and requires a development plant. The gasification systems produce gas from the coal feedstock which is then burned in a gas turbine/steam turbine combined cycle. Pf systems on the other hand burn the coal to raise steam in a boiler. The steam then passes directly through a steam turbine. Pf plant has been used to generate electricity for many years, and has developed in an incremental way. Recent developments have increased steam temperatures and pressures whilst keeping the cycles essentially the same. In identifying the R&D programme, the incremental nature of advanced pf development has been taken into account, so that improvements in subcritical plant are included along with consideration of supercritical plant. This will enable UK industry to maintain and increase its share of the cleaner coal market, during the continuing R&D programme.

The market for coal plant

World Market

A report on the market opportunities for coal-fired power plant was published on behalf of the International Energy Agency (IEA) in 1996 by the UK DTI (ref. 9). The report gives a breakdown of future markets by regions of the world and power plant type. As referred to above, 70% of the market has been projected to be in Asia. The market potential (in GW_e) in the 15-year period between 1995 and 2010 for new equipment identified by power plant type is given in the following table:

Table A1 - Market potential for power plant types

Technology	PF	AFBC[1]	PFBC[2]	Gasification[3]	Total New
Market potential (GW_e)	359-452	32-45	11-20	28-46	430-560

1 Atmospheric fluidised bed combustion   2 Pressurised fluidised bed combustion   3 Includes ABGC and IGCC

In this table, ABGC and IGCC figures are taken together. With regard to the other technologies, the view of the Foresight Task Force was that AFBC and PFBC plant are not current UK strengths and do not at present warrant such major attention for development by UK industry. AFBC technology is catered for, as a circulating FBC is an integral part of the ABGC. The figures predict that conventional and advanced pf plant will dominate with between 80% and 83% of the market. On the same figures ABGC and IGCC combined will share between 6% and 8% of the market over the 15-year timescale of the study.

Since the IEA study was carried out there has been a substantial drop in the price of plant, nearly 40% in the case of advanced pf and more than 20% for IGCC. Along with the change in the £/$ exchange rate, these reductions have affected the projected size of the market when measured in £billion. A comparison of the figures from the IEA study and more recent figures taken from a paper by Torrens (ref. 10) and an article by Chambers (ref. 11), for advanced pf and IGCC respectively, are given below, using an exchange rate of £1=$1.6 for the more recent figures:

Technology	Advanced pf + clean-up	Gasification*
IEA study	890	1133
Torrens/Chambers figures	560	890**

* includes ABGC and IGCC   ** mid-range figure

The cost of AFBC and PFBC plant appears to be falling at the same rate as advanced pf plant. Applying the Torrens/Chambers figures to the projected market (in GW$_e$) from the IEA study gives the following market potential for cleaner coal plant:

Technology	PF	AFBC	PFBC	Gasification*	Total New
Market potential (£billion)	201-253	18-25	6-11	25-41	249-328
Mid estimate (£billion)	227	21.5	8.5	33	290

* includes ABGC and IGCC

UK Market Share

In order to try and estimate the cost benefit to the UK of the technology R&D programmes described in the report, an estimate has to be made of the UK share of the worldwide market for the selected power plant types, advanced pf, ABGC and IGCC.

The world market for power plant as a whole has been increasing steadily (ref. 12) but over the last 3 years the UK share (ref. 5) has fallen from around 12.5% in 1995 to a (projected) 11% in 1997. Although accurate figures for market share are notoriously difficult to calculate it is clear that the UK share has dropped recently, and prompt action is required to maintain and increase UK market share in this sector.

For advanced pf, it seems reasonable to assume that if the UK maintains a strong presence in the market, then UK companies could expect to achieve 10% of the market in the future, even against a background of the UK share falling in the last few years.

The market figures for gasification plant given in Table A3 include both ABGC and IGCC technologies. Studies of the impact of a successful demonstration of ABGC technology have shown that ABGC could expect to take 8% of the total gasification market. Taking into account the strong position of UK industry in ABGC technology development, the UK could expect to take two-thirds of the ABGC market, giving 5.3% of the IGCC market with ABGC equipment. The UK could also expect to take around 10% of the remaining 92% (9.2%) of the gasification market. These figures for market share are translated into market value in Table A4 below, for advanced pf, ABGC and IGCC over a 15 year period. It has been assumed that the UK market share of these technologies includes not only the supply of turnkey plant but also components and systems.

In addition to the supply of new plant, UK industry has a strong position in spares and repairs. As with many capital industries, there is a trend towards plant manufacturers undertaking service contracts to maintain plant supplied to utilities and independent power producers (IPPs), and this is expected to become a growing share of the suppliers' businesses.

Two approaches have been taken to estimate the size of the spares and repairs business. From a utility point of view it is estimated that spares and repairs for existing plant are around 1%/annum of the initial capital cost of a plant, producing a total figure of between 20% and 30% depending on plant life. An alternative estimate of boiler maintenance cost, gives a figure of around 2%/annum. From a manufacturer's point of view an estimate can be made of the spares and repairs business as a proportion of annual turnover.

These figures can vary from year to year but fall mainly in the range 20-25%. There are of course no figures yet available for power plant types described in this report, but as a key technology target is to achieve RAMO (reliability, availability, maintainability, operability) exceeding current best practice, an estimate of spares and repairs business on future plant can be based on the historical figures above. Taking the above figures into account, then a realistic estimate of spares and repairs business could be around 20% of initial plant capital cost and this figure has been used in Table A4 to add to the figures for UK market share assuming UK industry obtains the same share of the spares and repairs business as the share of new plant.

Finally in the pf market there is the potential for the retrofit of cleaner coal technologies (removal of NO_x, SO_2 and particulates from existing plant). The IEA report estimates this at around 10% of the pf market. UK industry could be realistically expected to take a 10% share of this retrofit market also.

Table A4 - Mid-range estimate of expected UK market share including spares and repairs

Technology	PF	Gasification		Total
		ABGC	IGCC	
Mid estimate market potential (£billion)	227.0	33.0		260.0
UK market share (%)	10.0	5.3	9.2	
Mid estimate of market obtained by UK (£billion)	22.7	1.8	3.0	27.5
Spares & repairs @ 20%	4.5	0.4	0.6	5.5
Retrofit @ 10%	2.3			2.3
Total UK market share (£billion)	29.5	2.2	3.6	35.3

The Structure of the Project

The primary responsibility for drawing up the R,D&D programme for the power plant types was allocated between the project partners in the following way:

Advanced pf - International Combustion Ltd (now ABB Combustion Services Ltd)
   - Mitsui Babcock Energy Ltd
   - GEC ALSTHOM PGD (now ALSTOM Energy)

ABGC - GEC ALSTHOM PGD (now ALSTOM Energy)

IGCC - PowerGen plc

Developments required to satisfy the technology targets were identified for each power plant type and their key components. The R&D programmes required to provide the information necessary to allow the components to be designed, manufactured and tested were then drawn up for each power plant type and estimates made of the programme costs and timescales. The three programmes were evaluated and a cost/benefit analysis carried out for each power plant type. Consideration was also given to the need for appropriate demonstration plant. Conclusions were drawn from the analysis and recommendations made for the implementation of the R,D&D programme.

Meeting with Academics

A meeting between the project partners and invited academics was held at the DTI Conference Centre on 3 November 1997 to discuss R,D&D needs for cleaner coal technology. The partners presented the technology objectives of the project and the academics responded by submitting suggestions for R&D projects. Nearly 50 potential research proposals were identified as a result of this meeting.

The R&D programmes

The R&D programmes for the three power plant types, advanced pf, ABGC and IGCC, are listed, described and discussed below in some detail. The individual programme tasks were allocated a high, medium or low priority, to give an indication of their importance to the components and plant for which they are required. High priority projects are those without which the technology would not be able to achieve the targets set. Medium and low priority projects relate to R&D required for plant to remain competitive, low priority being applied to long-term projects and/or less important components. The R&D programme for each power plant type is summarised in the following Sections. For advanced pf the programme continues the incremental nature of the R&D to meet the technology targets. For IGCC the programme covers all the work required to improved capital cost, reliability and flexibility, and the ABGC R&D programme is that required to get a plant operational at the minimum R&D cost.

Advanced PF

The use of pulverised coal as a primary energy source for electricity generation is long established and the maturity of the technology, to a large extent, influences the nature of the R,D&D programme required to ensure that UK industry remains as a viable player in the world marketplace. Here the emphasis is on incremental developments to improve steam conditions, increase overall plant efficiency, reduce costs (both capital and operating), and ensure compliance with environmental legislation.

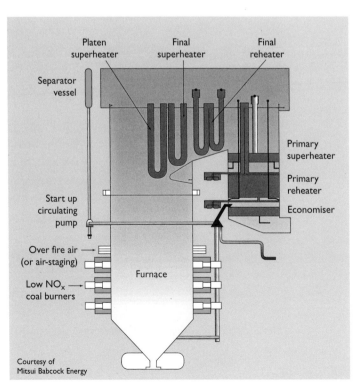

A schematic of an advanced supercritical pf boiler

Courtesy of Mitsui Babcock Energy

Meri-Pori advanced supercritical pf plant in Finland, which is based on a Mitsui Babcock Energy Ltd design

Courtesy of IVO International

The key areas where R,D&D effort is required can be summarised as follows:

- materials;
- NO_x control and associated issues;
- improvements to plant components;
- underpinning sciences.

The attainment of steam conditions of 375bar/700°C or higher are dependent upon the successful development and deployment of some components manufactured from nickel-based alloys, including superheaters, headers, pipework, steam chests, rotors and turbine casings. Nickel is, however, a highly expensive commodity and hence further developments and optimisation of high temperature steels are also required in parallel to maximise their use and minimise the cost within such advanced plant. For all these materials, major developments are required in fabrication techniques to identify appropriate weld procedures, obtain code approvals and carry out component demonstrations in plant environments.

Other materials development issues relate to corrosion resistance (both high and low temperature) and improvements in wear properties in the milling/pf transport system.

NO_x emissions arising from the combustion of coal in pf systems can be significant unless specific measurements are taken to control this. Whilst low emissions to atmosphere can be achieved by tail-end processes (ie SCR) it is generally more cost-effective to minimise the NO_x levels exiting the boiler. Here the R,D&D programme aims to further develop in-furnace NO_x reduction techniques, the programme also takes into account the important related issues of carbon in ash, slagging and fouling, and high temperature corrosion.

Recent developments
in technologies at
Mitsui Babcock
Energy Ltd to reduce
NO$_x$ emissions from
pf plant

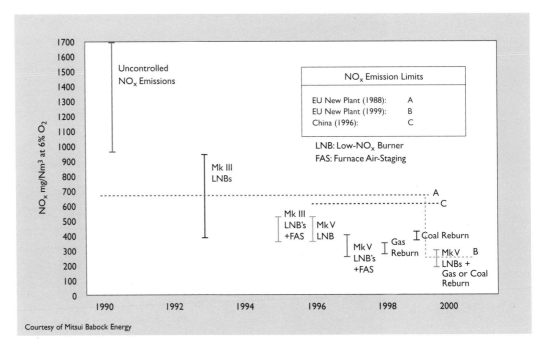

Courtesy of Mitsui Babock Energy

Incremental improvements to the individual components to improve reliability and reduce cost will continue to be made. Associated with this is the development of better predictive tools based upon an improved understanding of the processes occurring. As well as specific hardware developments, the use of advanced control methodologies (ie expert systems, condition monitoring) can also lead to improved plant performance by allowing operation at optimum conditions and pre-emptive maintenance to be completed before equipment failure occurs - the use of these techniques is to be extended to a wider range of power plant applications.

A necessary step to the development of improved predictive tools, and in particular those for combustion, slagging and fouling, milling and pf transport, is a good understanding of the processes occurring. Measurement techniques need to be based upon the realistic simulation of the relevant process (eg high temperatures and heating rates during coal devolatilisation), non-invasive, and capable of replication by competent laboratories. Better models to describe the processes occurring need to be developed, and they must be validated against data which is of industrial significance.

Much of the R&D programme is of equal value to both subcritical and supercritical plant. There are a number of activities which are essential to the advancement of the steam conditions (ie materials) but these also benefit plant having less onerous requirements in that components such as headers can be produced with thinner walls (lower susceptibility to long-term creep and fatigue damage).

Flue gas desulphurisation (FGD) is a mature technology and an integral component of advanced pf plant. Improvements will be incremental in nature and cover materials development, availability and maintenance issues, and running and disposal costs among others.

The table below summarises the costs of the advanced pf R&D programme, in terms of the technology areas and the priorities.

Table A5 - Advanced pf R&D programme by technology area

Technology Area	High Priority £k	Medium Priority £k	Low Priority £k	Total £k
Coal science	8,000	9,275	1,450	18,725
Combustion	7,900	200		8,100
Component design and development	24,650	5,300	4,200	34,150
Control and instrumentation	8,050	1,200		9,250
Fluid flow and heat transfer	8,500	500	9,400	18,400
Integration, optimisation and modelling	12,575	3,240	2,700	18,515
Materials and lifing	102,800	4,500		107,300
Total (£k)	172,475	24,215	17,750	214,440

ABGC

The ABGC power plant is a hybrid, advanced cleaner coal technology in which the solid feedstock is gasified in an air-blown spouted fluidised bed gasifier to produce a fuel suitable for a gas turbine. The feedstock is not completely converted in the gasifier and the resultant solid product from the gasifier (char) is passed to a circulating fluidised bed combustor (CFBC) where the feedstock burnout is completed.

The R&D programme is required to support the demonstrator plant and future developments. Major requirements for R&D fall into the following areas:

- gasification;
- chemistry and catalysis;
- materials;
- coal science.

In an ABGC, some emission control is carried out in the gasifier using chemical sorbents to remove sulphur. This leads to complex high temperature reactions and R&D is required to improve fuel gas production and improve sulphur capture. The basic behaviour of coal in the gasifier has effects on all downstream operations of the plant and requires continuing investigation. Gasifier performance using waste and biomass and the behaviour of mixtures and blends are all important areas of study.

Hot gas clean up (HGCU) is also a complex process. The performance of ceramic materials used in the construction of the filter elements is important together with the mechanical and chemical behaviour of particulates. Developments to control halides and ammonia in the HGCU is a major area for chemistry R&D.

Materials behaviour in all areas of the cycle requires further investigation, particularly during start up and down time. It is important that materials able to withstand gas flows with reduced contaminant removal are developed for gas turbine components in order to improve the reliability of the plant. Key materials problems also occur in areas where the transport of solids occurs.

The gasifier will be able to operate on a wide range of low quality feedstocks including biomass and sewage sludge together with coals with a high ash content. The CFBC will be able to operate on any mixture of char and original feedstock. These two features significantly improve the adaptability and operability of the ABGC allowing the plant to deliver nearly full-rated power whilst the gasifier is out of operation for maintenance, for example.

At this time, the major novel component technologies have been developed and demonstrated individually in large test rigs and the work is ongoing. The need for a demonstrator plant is recognised and an effort is under way to specify such a plant and to identify the funding and procedures required for its establishment.

Much of the future development work will hinge on the experience gained from the demonstrator plant and might indeed be carried out using the demonstrator plant. The need to carry out development work using the demonstrator will be reflected in the design of the plant. It is hoped that the demonstrator will start to be commissioned within the next five years and it is estimated that, at the planned size of $90MW_e$, the capital cost will be about £120 million.

It is anticipated that the successful demonstration of the ABGC will permit acceptance of the technology such that subsequent plant will be established on commercial terms to answer the needs of markets. These markets are considered to be particularly in India and the Far East where coal is expected to be a major energy source of the future and where the indigenous coals, whilst abundant, contain a lot of ash. The ABGC needs to be available so that the United Kingdom can export the technology to satisfy the increasing power demands and growing environmental concerns in India and the Far East.

Because no demonstrator exists yet for the ABGC it is very difficult to be prescriptive when forecasting its future development needs. In producing the data provided within this report, the progress of the technology to date has been taken into account along with reports from and discussions with the various workers in the field. Table A6 lists the various areas which require work, either to drive towards the required operating performance or to reduce technical and hence commercial risk.

The cost of the ABGC R&D programme is £58 million over a ten-year period. This is in addition to the cost of £120 million for the $90MW_e$ demonstrator, which is an integral part of the overall ABGC development programme.

Technology Area	High Priority £k	Medium Priority £k	Low Priority £k	Total £k
Coal science	1,000	5,400	1,000	7,400
Combustion and gasification	5,000	7,700		12,700
Component design and development		1,200	4,000	5,200
Control and instrumentation		1,400	2,000	3,400
Fluid flow and heat transfer		400	4,000	4,400
Materials and lifing	2,000	2,800	2,200	7,000
Chemistry and catalysis	7,000	6,000	2,600	15,600
Integration, optimisation and modelling		1,400	1,000	2,400
Total £k	15,000	26,300	16,800	58,100

Note: Costings carried out on basis of minimum R&D programme to get a demonstration plant running

IGGC

IGCC is a relatively new technology, but there is sufficient experience of demonstration plant worldwide to determine its current status. IGCC is very clean and efficient; with the adoption of the more advanced H-class gas turbine technology, IGCCs should comfortably exceed 50% efficiency. However, at the present time, IGCCs are more expensive to build than conventional coal-fired plant and their reliability and operational flexibility still need to be demonstrated. Fuel flexibility with coal has also to be fully proven. Large IGCC plant projected for operation from 1999 onwards are using a variety of fuels including petroleum coke, oil residues and sewage sludge (ref. 11). The British Gas (BG)/Lurgi gasifier has a particular advantage for waste applications since, unlike most other gasifiers, it can accommodate feedstocks with large particle sizes. The slagging system ensures that mineral matter present in the waste material is incorporated into the inert slag.

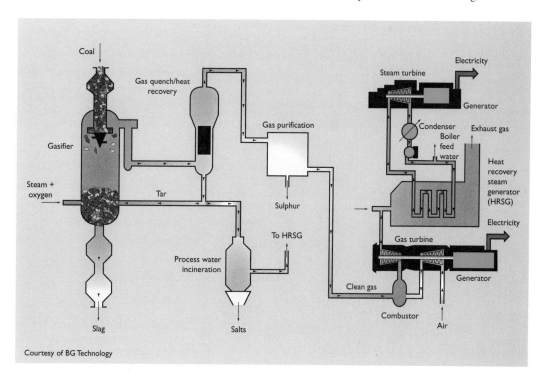

A schematic of the
British Gas/Lurgi
IGCC

Courtesy of BG Technology

R&D priorities for IGCC are clearly to reduce capital costs and improve reliability and operability, and, to a lesser extent, to establish fuel flexibility. R&D into further improving IGCC's environmental performance or efficiency is not a priority and no work in these areas is recommended in this report.

The main areas of IGCC technology into which R&D is required are:

- gasification fundamentals;
- improvement of individual plant components;
- overall plant optimisation.

Research in the fundamentals of gasification is required to establish the fuel flexibility of IGCC technologies. Much of this work would be undertaken by universities and would be directed at understanding gasification reaction rates and carbon conversion and predicting the gasifiability of individual coals. This work is of high to medium priority.

R&D is required to improve the following components of IGCC to make them more reliable and/or cheaper:

- gasifiers/syngas coolers;
- pressurised coal feeding systems;
- gas clean-up;
- gas turbines;
- air separation units.

The required R&D for gasifiers and syngas coolers is centred on the development of improved alloys and manufacturing processes to improve the corrosion resistance and lower the cost of these components. Both industry and universities would have an important part to play. This work has a high priority.

Pressurised coal feeding systems (both dry pf systems and briquetting systems) need to be improved to increase reliability and lower costs. This is medium priority work.

The development of improved hot gas clean-up systems could lower the cost of IGCC by providing a cheaper alternative to the conventional, low-temperature processes currently employed. R&D is required to improve the reliability of both hot gas filter and hot gas desulphurisation systems. This is a medium priority area involving both industry and universities.

The highest priority gas turbine R&D for IGCC is the development of better combustion systems for low calorific value (CV) syngas. Studies of NO_x formation are also required, although these are only medium priority. Also required is the development of more rugged gas turbines, capable of reliable running on unclean or partly clean syngas: this is medium priority work. Whereas the work on low CV syngas combustion will involve both industry and universities in collaboration, it is likely that the development of the more rugged gas turbines will be undertaken by industry alone.

ALSTOM Energy's gas turbine combustor test facility

ALSTOM Energy's Frame 9F gas turbine

Further work is required to allow the successful integration of air separation units (ASUs) into an IGCC. The two areas requiring attention are improved control systems for, and better dynamic simulation of, highly integrated ASUs. This is high priority work which could involve both industry and universities. There is also the need, in the longer-term, for alternatives to conventional cryogenic ASUs in order to lower costs.

A key area of R&D for IGCC is optimisation of the overall plant configuration and layout. This is a high priority area, in which universities could play a key role. Specific issues which require study are:

- dynamic simulation;
- start-up and shut-down strategies;
- operability;

- simplified designs which reduce cost;
- optimum integration strategies;
- combining operability assessments within existing thermo-economic optimisation techniques.

Table A7 below summarises the costs of the IGCC R&D Programme, broken down into priorities and key technology areas. Because there is considerable overlap between the R&D needs for IGCC and those for other cleaner coal technologies (such as the ABGC) and other technology areas (eg natural-gas-fired CCGTs, ASUs) some of the R&D required for IGCC is better covered under other programmes. Table A7 therefore indicates the gross programme costs, the cost element attributable to other programme areas and the net cost attributable to this IGCC programme, to cover improvements to capital cost, reliability and flexibility.

Table A7 – IGCC R&D programme by technology areas

Technology Area	High Priority (£million)			Medium Priority (£million)			Low Priority (£million)			Total (£million)		
	Gross	Attributable	Net	Gross	Attributable	Net	Gross	Attributable	Net	Gross	Attributable	Net
Coal science	2		2	2		2	3		3	7		7
Combustion	5		5	2		2				7		7
Component design and development				77	42	35	100	100		177	142	35
Control and instrumentation	5		5							5		5
Fluid flow and heat transfer				1	1					1	1	
Materials and lifing	35		35	40	15	25				75	15	60
Chemistry and catalysis				7	7					7	7	
Integration, optimisation and modelling	12		12				4		4	16		16
Total (£million)	59		59	129	65	64	107	100	7	295	165	130

Gross — Estimated cost of total R&D programme

Attributable - R&D attributable to other programmes

Net — Cost attributable to this IGCC programme

Cost-Effectiveness of the R&D Programmes

The overall cost-effectiveness of each programme can be gauged in terms of the R&D costs summarised in Table A8 and the market figures in Table A4.

Table A8 – R&D costs for the power plant types

Power Plant Type	Overall R&D Costs (£k)			
	High Priority	Medium Priority	Low Priority	Total
Advanced pf	172,475	24,215	17,750	214,440
ABGC	15,000	26,300	16,800	*58,100
IGCC	59,000	64,000	7,000	130,000
Total	246,475	114,515	41,550	402,540

* Excludes the cost of the Prototype Integrated Plant demonstrator

The overall high cost of the IGCC programme compared with the ABGC programme reflects the fact that IGCC is a generic technology covering a number of different gasifier systems whereas ABGC is a single, clearly defined system. If UK industry was to identify a preferred IGCC type, eg the BG/Lurgi system, then the IGCC R&D programme would be reviewed in the light of that decision.

Using these figures a cost/benefit analysis can be carried out for the R&D programmes for each of the three power plant types:

Plant Type	UK Market Share (£ million)	R&D Programme Cost (£ million)	R&D Cost as % of UK market share
Advanced pf	29,500	214.4	0.73
ABGC	2,200	*58.1	2.64
IGCC	3,600	130.0	3.61

* Excludes the cost of the Prototype Integrated Plant demonstrator

If the high priority programme for IGCC is combined with the high and medium priority programmes of ABGC and the total advanced pf programme, the total spend is £314.7 million over a 20 year period, (see Table A10) the cost/benefit of each of the programmes falls below 2% and the cost/benefit of the whole cleaner coal R&D programme is below 1%. This will provide a very cost-effective cleaner coal R&D programme for UK industry. The low priority activities of the ABGC are in the longer-term part of the programme, and can be left until a later date, and the medium and low priority activities of the IGCC programme can be picked up under other R&D programmes.

Power Plant Type	Estimated Size of UK Market Share (£million)	R&D Priorities Selected	R&D cost (£ million)	R&D Cost as % of market
Advanced pf	29,500	All	214.4	0.73
ABGC	2,200	High & Medium	41.3	1.88
IGCC	3,600	High	59.0	1.64
Total	35,300	-	314.7	0.89

Annual Cost of R&D Programmes

The R&D programmes for the power plant types have been identified to meet the market timescales given in Table A10. The spend in the first five years of the 20-year programme is shown in Figure A1 but it is unlikely that the programme could reach such a high level of spend in the first year. However the first five years of the R&D programme (£176 million) could be completed if the spend profile increased from a starting figure of £32 million in the first year to a rate of £36 million/annum over the next four years. This spend profile is also shown in Figure A1. The breakdown of costs by technology area for the four-year programme is given in Table A11, with a similar proportion of spend allocation in the first year.

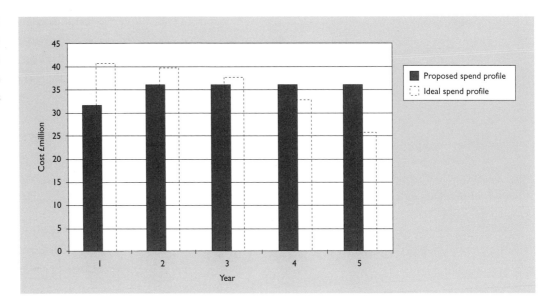

Figure A1. Annual cost of R&D programmes total £176 million over five years

Table A11 - Annual R&D spend by technology area

Technology Area	Total (£million)	%
Coal science	3.10	8.6
Combustion and gasification	2.95	8.2
Component design and development	4.03	11.2
Control and instrumentation	1.58	4.4
Fluid flow and heat transfer	2.16	6.0
Materials and lifing	16.81	46.7
Chemistry and catalysis	1.48	4.1
Integration, optimisation and modelling	3.89	10.8
Total (£million/annum)	36.00	100

It is difficult to propose specific R&D programmes beyond this timescale and a review will be necessary to consider progress towards the technology objectives and changes in the market-place. A thorough review of progress should be carried out annually, with a major evaluation in Year 4 to set the programme for the following five years. The evaluation should not only assess progress on the R&D programmes, but also any shifts in markets and/or technology objectives.

Technologies

The R&D programmes are described in detail in the main report. Some examples are given below of the types of R&D required, under the technology areas in Table A11 above. The list is not exhaustive and it is the intention that the successor organisation to the Clean Coal Task Force will review, update and co-ordinate the R&D programmes for advanced pf, ABGC and IGCC.

Coal Science
Advanced pf
- new uses for ash
- effect on ash of clean-up technologies
- impact of coal quality on turndown, burnout and NO_X formation

	•	acquisition of data on and modelling of combustion performance of coals
ABGC	•	evaluation of calcium deposits
	•	characterisation of "sticky" dust
IGCC	•	prediction of carbon conversion
	•	empirical tests for gasification characteristics

Combustion and Gasification

Advanced pf	•	NO_x reduction – integration of boiler and burners, development of improved and novel processes
	•	improvement of mixing technologies
	•	extension of wall firing to lower-volatile coals
	•	modelling of flame furnace interactions
ABGC	•	control of ammonia production
	•	explosion control
	•	gas turbine combustor developments, modelling and testing of low calorific value gases (from ABGC process)
	•	syngas characterisation
IGCC	•	research into gasification fundamentals
	•	gas turbine developments, modelling, and testing of low calorific value gases (from IGCC processes)

Component Design and Development

Advanced pf	•	improve mechanical design of fuel feed system
	•	low NO_x burner design, novel concepts, integration of design with integrated reburn and NO_x reduction processes, greater robustness to fuel quality changes
	•	improved design tools for furnace, superheaters, reheaters, headers, pipework, steam turbine/generators & FGD
ABGC	•	Novel concepts for high temperature fuel valves develop engineering from small demonstration plant to full-scale commercial plant

Control and Instrumentation

Advanced pf	•	develop methods for on-line analysis of coal size, component wear/replacement strategy for mill components;
	•	improved flame monitoring techniques
	•	external condition monitoring for wider range of plant components and integrate whole plant condition monitoring system
	•	application of advanced control methodologies

ABGC	• syngas online monitoring
	• improved control and instrumentation for integration of hot gas clean-up
	• dynamic simulation of whole plant
	• develop dedicated reliability, availability and maintainability model
IGCC	• dynamic simulation of whole plant
	• improve start-up and shut-down cycles

Fluid Flow and Heat Transfer

Advanced pf	• acquisition of fundamental heat transfer data for furnaces
	• develop understanding of deposition processes on tubes
	• improved flow distribution between superheater elements
	• improved flow models for steam turbines
	• improved cooling methodologies for generators
ABGC	• improved flow in hot gas clean-up components

Materials and Lifing

Advanced pf	• improved materials for milling and pulverising plant and fuel supply lines
	• lifing methodologies for vibrating components, balls and rollers in coal beds
	• improved understanding of wear mechanisms
	• improved models for corrosion prediction in furnaces
	• improved materials for furnaces, headers, superheaters, reheaters, high pressure and low pressure turbine rotors, casings, blading, pipework
	• improved weld and fabrication methods
	• novel materials and manufacturing techniques (eg composite pipes etc)
ABGC	• improved methods for assessing erosion and deposition effects on materials
	• in-situ rainbow testing of selected materials
	• lifing methodologies for maintenance and outage periods
IGCC	• establish corrosion resistance of alloys and refractories in gasifiers
	• development of improved alloys and refractories in gasifiers
	• corrosion resistance of alloys and coatings in syngas coolers
	• develop improved materials, coatings and manufacturing techniques for syngas coolers
	• develop cheaper manufacturing processes

Chemistry and Catalysis

ABGC
- integrated halide and sulphur removal
- selective oxidisation of ammonia (NH_3)
- impact of above on desulphurisation and NH_3 downstream conversion
- de-dusting

Integration Optimisation and Modelling

Advanced pf
- integration and optimisation of rope destructors
- modelling of flame shapes/lengths, effect of turndown on flames, validation of mathematical models
- improved computational fluid dynamics models for burners
- develop slagging models and rules for slagging avoidance
- methods for techno-economic assessment of steam cycles, optimisation of cycle
- optimise disposition of heating surfaces to reduce supercritical fabrication costs
- minimisation of pipe runs
- integration of FGD system, optimisation and modelling

ABGC
- site influence on optimisation of plant layout
- optimisation of auxiliary air compressor requirements

IGCC
- requirements and capability of operability
- techno-economic evaluation of operability
- development of optimum integration strategies
- improved dynamic simulation of integrated plant
- optimisation of operation and control of plant

Funding sources and management plan

Funding for the programme will come from a combination of the following sources:

a) UK industry;

b) UK Government (eg a continuation of the DTI's Cleaner Coal Technology Programme, EPSRC, collaborative programmes with other Foresight panels);

c) European Union (Framework 5 Programme);

d) Other international collaborative programmes (through eg IEA and bilateral programmes).

The co-ordination of the programme will be a significant undertaking and a successor organisation to the Clean Coal Task Force should be set up to take this forward. The organisation should be industry-led, say through a trade association, and include representatives of Government, industry and academia. Creating an appropriate structure should be done as quickly as possible, but it will still take time. To maintain the momentum generated by this study it is necessary that R&D activity does not falter in the interim. For these reasons it is important that the DTI's Cleaner Coal Technology Programme continues to provide continuity in Government support for R&D in the UK and confidence within the partners in this project, so that all the work carried out so far under Foresight will not be lost through lack of appropriate encouragement.

The R&D programme described is the best estimate that can be made at this time. It may be possible to reduce costs by close co-ordination of the R&D programmes of the power plant types and the R&D programme arising from the parallel study into combined cycle and gas turbine technology requirements. There will also be the opportunity for collaboration across sector boundaries, industrial gas turbines and aero engines being a good example of collaboration between the Power Plant Sector and the Defence and Aerospace Sector. Over time the R&D programme will need revising and the Task Force should take this into account when it draws up its co-ordination plan.

The R&D programme described above has an annual expenditure in excess of £36 million/annum (once it is fully under way).

Plant demonstration

The demonstration of full-size components and complete power plant is the essential step between a successful R&D programme and commercial exploitation of new technology.

Advanced PF

Technology developments in advanced pf plant are clearly identified as incremental and, as R&D results become available to enable the demonstration of new types of equipment, some of the new components will be introduced into an appropriate power station. R&D and component developments have been timed to meet the objectives set by the Task Force, for commercially competitive plant achieving over 50% efficiency between 2010 and 2020. However the opportunity to increase efficiencies for advanced pf plant beyond 50%, continuing in an incremental way, is included in the R,D&D programme.

Although UK companies have been successful in demonstrating improved technologies in world markets on this basis, because of the recent emphasis in the UK on gas-fired combined cycle plant, no new coal-fired power station has been built since the completion of Drax in 1985. This has resulted in UK companies lacking a large, domestic supercritical, coal-fired power plant to demonstrate components, such as new boilers and turbines, to external customers in a single demonstrator. The industry has the capability to design and build such a plant which would provide a focus for the continuing R&D and be a stepping stone for the planned advances to plant of even higher pressure and temperature.

At the present time UK companies are involved in a THERMIE project evaluating the prospects for two advanced pf plant operating at 700°C, one at $400MW_e$ and one at $1,000MW_e$. The approximate cost of a $400MW_e$ demonstration plant would be around £225 million and a $1,000MW_e$ plant would cost around £560 million. Such a plant would generate electricity more cheaply than new power stations based on existing coal-fired technology and would satisfy the lower emission limits being considered for large combustion plant. A $1,000MW_e$ plant would allow a large boiler and steam turbine to be demonstrated but may not be feasible in the UK market because of the unit flexibility required by the electricity market.

ABGC

The R&D programme set out for the ABGC leads to the demonstration of a Prototype Integrated Plant (PIP), as an intermediate step in the development of the technology. An extension of the R&D programme beyond that will assist in the demonstration of the viability of a complete ABGC, for sale into the market-place. The initial need is for a complete and fully integrated plant to demonstrate the concept at a suitable scale in order to give customer confidence that a full-scale commercial plant can be constructed and operated successfully. Because of the smaller scale of a demonstration PIP, the specific cost will be high, so that a PIP at around 90MW$_e$ is likely to cost in the region of £120 million.

IGCC

A number of IGCC plant using coal are already operating, although none has yet been able to operate without subsidy. The BG/Lurgi technology is to be used at a plant in Westfield, Scotland, to convert sewage sludge to syngas, and also in a coal and waste gasification power plant in Germany. The options for a UK demonstration of IGCC technology are for a demonstrator early in the next century (IGCC-2000), or later (IGCC-2010). The early demonstrator would be based on existing technology, risking the unreliability of existing IGCC demonstrators. It would, however, give an early demonstration of the BG/Lurgi technology in power generation, and provide continuity with the Westfield plant. A later demonstrator would have a greater chance of success benefiting from the results of the R&D programme and indications of whether the projected market for IGCC is developing as expected. A 300MW$_e$ demonstration of IGCC technology is likely to cost in the region of £500 million, a figure based on the published cost of similar demonstrator IGCC plant in the US Department of Energy Clean Coal Technology Demonstration Program.

A summary of the projected capital cost of demonstration power plant for each of the three power plant types is shown in the table below:

Table A12 - Cost of demonstration power plant

Plant Type	Output (MW$_e$)	Cost (£million)
Advanced pf	400/1,000	225/560
ABGC	90	120
IGCC	300	500

The figures given in Table A12 are for demonstrator plant only and are additional to the costs of the R&D programmes previously described. None of these plant would be expected to generate electricity on a commercial basis, and therefore each would require an element of financial subsidy, the actual amount depending on a number of factors including its location, the accepted reliability of the plant and an estimate of the basic cost of electricity on the grid at the time of operation.

Other research programmes

The present report has drawn on proposals for cleaner coal R&D programmes, not only in the UK and Europe, but also in the US and elsewhere. In the UK a major study on materials for cleaner coal plant has been put forward to the Foresight Energy and Materials Panels. The Energy Panel Task Force on Advanced Combined Cycle and Gas Turbine Technology has recently commissioned an R,D&D study similar to the present study. The Defence and Aerospace Panel has produced a number of R&D reports; the ones relating to technology programmes in aerodynamics, materials and structures, integrated systems and sensors all have relevance to requirements for Cleaner Coal R&D Programmes.

The Coal Industry Advisory Board of the IEA has published a report on the factors affecting the take-up of cleaner coal technologies (ref. 13). This report dealt not only with technology matters but also with the conservatism of the utility industry and its reluctance to take up new technology. This is likely to be exacerbated in those parts of the world where the supply of electricity is being deregulated. To overcome this attitude requires persistence on the part of suppliers and stresses the vital importance of demonstration plant and good working relationships between manufacturers and utilities.

In the USA, cleaner coal R&D is focused and supported through the Clean Coal Technology Demonstration Program of the US Department of Energy (USDOE). Projects include the demonstration of complete IGCC plant but also other cleaner coal technology components such as SO_2 and NO_X control. According to the USDOE, the projects have shown the capability to meet the required environmental performance and will be capable of meeting the operational and economic performance necessary to compete in the market-place. The total programme cost over the ten-year period has been at the rate of around £320 million/annum. The power generation part of this programme is valued at £200 million/annum with the USDOE contribution amounting to almost 40% of the total.

Recommendations

In order to meet the Foresight R,D&D priorities for cleaner coal technologies set out in this Summary Report the following recommendations are made:

a)   The five year R&D programmes described above should be commenced as soon as possible. **The value of the programme should be £32 million in the first year, rising to £36 million/annum for the following four years** to enable commercially competitive plant to enter the market-place between 2010 and 2020. Funding for the programme will come from a combination of sources.

b)   The Cleaner Coal Technology Programme of the DTI should continue, with emphasis on the technology programmes set out in this report, to maintain continuity and provide a structure within which UK industry can continue to work together, and with academia.

c)   The emphasis of the cleaner coal technology activity in the UK should be on power generation technologies and be an integral part of an advanced power generation programme embracing other key technologies for the UK, in particular those relevant to gas turbines operating on a wide range of fuels.

d)   A structure should be set up as soon as possible to enable the R&D programme to progress effectively and bring together the various sources of funding to maximise the benefit to UK industry. Within the structure should be a mechanism to carry out a thorough review of progress on the R&D programmes on an annual basis, with a major evaluation of the programme priorities, including any shifts in markets and/or technology targets, in Year 4.

e)   Government, equipment manufacturers and generators should enter discussions to provide the mechanisms for the funding of advanced power generation technology demonstrators. Establishment of such demonstrators will be essential to assist the export of the technologies to appropriate global markets.

Annex B

Status of Cleaner Coal Technologies

This Annex briefly summarises the status of the key cleaner coal technologies used for electricity generation. It is not meant to be an exhaustive technical assessment of the merits of each technology. More detailed assessment of the technologies can be found in the excellent reports published by IEA Coal Research - The Clean Coal Centre. Details of the reports are available from its internet site (http://www.iea.coal.org.uk).

Introduction

Cleaner coal technologies, in general, include all technologies which have been/are being developed and used to enhance both the efficiency and the environmental performance of coal extraction, preparation and utilisation, thus covering the complete coal cycle. However, the term is commonly used for technologies which are associated with power generation plant with a view to improving their efficiency of generation, reliability, availability and environmental performance. With recent developments in various cleaner coal technologies, there is a growing tendency in the developed countries to consider the minimum performance target of a clean coal power generation plant as follows :

Thermal efficiency of power generation	: 42% (lower heating value basis)
NO_x emissions	: 200mg Nm^{-3}
SO_2 emissions	: 200mg Nm^{-3}
Particulate emissions	: 25mg Nm^{-3}

Pulverised fuel combustion

Pulverised fuel (pf) combustion is the most widely used technique for utility power generation. The advent of legislation to reduce atmospheric pollution and the continuing requirement to be more cost-competitive have, over a long period, been the main drivers to development of the technology. Efficiency has been raised and environmental impact reduced through the use of higher steam conditions, more effective engineering design and the application of emissions control technologies.

Subcritical Steam Cycle

The efficiency of power generation based on conventional pf combustion using subcritical steam conditions (ie lower than 221.1bar, the critical pressure of steam) has increased over the years with gradual increase in both steam pressure and temperature. As a result, current operational UK subcritical steam cycle plant, using steam at around 190bar and 570°C, are achieving around 38% efficiency with FGD fitted. Higher efficiencies are now possible with more modern designs - around 41% with FGD, depending on cooling mechanisms (eg cooling towers or UK estuarine cooling). The properties of materials used in boilers and turbines have been the main problem in limiting further increase of steam conditions to achieve higher efficiencies.

Supercritical Steam Cycle

Taking advantage of developments in materials and associated fabrication technologies, supercritical steam cycles, using steam at around 240bar and 540-560°C, have been introduced from the early 1990s in countries such as Denmark, Germany, the Netherlands and Japan, achieving efficiencies around 43-45%. As a result, supercritical plant are now commercially available and are the preferred option, particularly in Japan and Denmark. Currently, over 40 supercritical plant are in operation worldwide, over 30 of which are in Japan (the Japanese plant are thought to have been all designed, engineered and manufactured in Japan). All of these plant are operating well with satisfactory performance and reliability.

Ultrasupercritical Steam Cycle

Development of new materials such as high-strength ferritic steels coupled with improved steam turbine design has recently allowed steam conditions to be raised further - to ultrasupercritical levels (note: as no precise physical definition applies for ultrasupercritical conditions, they are often defined as steam at >250bar and >570°C). As a result, two ultrasupercritical units, each rated at 400MW$_e$, have recently been built and commissioned in Denmark using steam at 285bar and 580°C, achieving 47% efficiency (at local conditions), and using internationally-traded coals. Extensive materials-related R&D activities are currently in progress in Europe, Japan and the USA with a view to developing advanced nickel-based alloys which would allow steam conditions at >300bar and >700°C and achieve efficiencies in excess of 50%. Such plant are expected to be demonstrated by the year 2010.

A comprehensive review of the current status of supercritical steam cycles has recently been published (ref. 14).

Emissions control technologies

NO$_x$ Control

To reduce NO$_x$ emissions, combustion modifications such as low-NO$_x$ burners and furnace air staging have been employed worldwide in about 380 and 120 coal-fired units, respectively, ie, in plant with total installed generation capacities of over 130GW$_e$ and over 50GW$_e$, respectively. Furnace fuel staging, or reburn, using natural gas as reburn fuel, is currently being demonstrated on a 600MW$_e$ unit at ScottishPower's Longannet Power Station, achieving 50% NO$_x$ reduction.

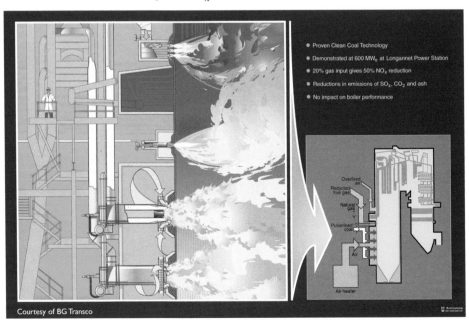

- Proven Clean Coal Technology
- Demonstrated at 600 MW$_e$ at Longannet Power Station
- 20% gas input gives 50% NO$_x$ reduction
- Reductions in emissions of SO$_x$, CO$_2$ and ash
- No impact on boiler performance

Courtesy of BG Transco

A schematic of the gas reburn system being used to reduce NO$_x$ at Longannet Power Station

Work is also in progress to demonstrate the use of coal as the reburn fuel. This is taking place on a 320MW$_e$ boiler at ENEL's Vado Ligure plant in Italy. Flue gas treatment-based NO$_x$-reduction technologies such as selective catalytic reduction (SCR) and selective non-catalytic reduction (SNCR) are also commercially available. SCR has been applied particularly widely in Japan and Germany to meet stringent NO$_x$ emission limits not achievable with combustion modifications. Japan and Germany have total installed generation capacities of about 30GW$_e$ and 15GW$_e$ respectively. The extent of NO$_x$ reduction achievable using these measures as indicated in Table B1.

Table B1- NO$_x$-reduction measures for pf combustion plant

Technology	% NO$_x$ reduction
Combustion modification:	
1. Low-NO$_x$ burners	30-60*
2. Furnace air-staging	20-40
3. 1 and 2 combined	50-60
4. Reburn	50-60
5. 1 and 4 combined	70
Flue gas treatment:	
1. SNCR	30-50
2. SCR	80-90

* up to 70% is now claimed for the latest designs of burners

Advanced intelligent control systems have also been developed and are being used to improve plant performance and reduce NO$_x$ emissions. For example, GNOCIS (generic NO$_x$ control intelligent system) has been developed in a UK and USA collaboration, and used successfully in several UK and US power plant to achieve significant NO$_x$ reduction while optimising plant performance.

Courtesy of PowerGen

The control room at Kingsnorth Power Station where GNOCIS has been implemented

Particulates Control

Electrostatic precipitators (ESPs) and fabric filters or "baghouses" are capable of removing >99.5% of particulates. ESPs have found wide application in Europe and in many other parts of the world. In the USA, however, both ESPs and fabric filters have been used, the selection being made to meet specific plant requirements.

Sulphur Dioxide Control

Various FGD processes such as wet scrubbing (including regenerable and non-regenerable processes), spray dry scrubbing and dry sorbent injection are commercially available for SO_2 removal. Wet scrubbing is the most widely used process and is capable of removing >95% of SO_2. Current total worldwide FGD installation capacity is around $150GW_e$, about 85% of which is based on non-regenerable wet scrubbers using mainly lime or limestone as the sorbent. Spray dry scrubbing accounts for about 10% of capacity while processes such as dry sorbent injection, and regenerable and combined SO_2/NO_x reduction account for the rest.

Courtesy of National Power

A view of National Power's $4,000MW_e$ Drax Power Station, which uses a wet scrubbing FGD process for SO_2 removal

Pressurised Fluidised Bed Combustion (PFBC)

PFBC units generate pressurised hot gas and steam from the combustion of fuel in fluidised beds using air under pressure. The steam is used in a conventional steam cycle. The hot pressurised gas leaving the bed at about 850°C is first cleaned of dust particles and then expanded through a gas turbine to generate additional electricity. In a typical PFBC system, about 80% of electricity is produced from the steam cycle and the rest from the gas turbine. Subcritical combined (gas and steam) cycle systems have an efficiency of 42-44% (at local conditions). Commercial-scale plant are now in operation in Sweden (Värtan), Spain (Escatron), and Japan (Wakamatsu and Tomato-Atsuma). Recently, PFBC units have also been ordered by Germany (Cottbus), China (Dalian) and Japan (one $250MW_e$ unit under construction and a second $250MW_e$ unit planned - both at Osaki Power Station). As with pf combustion, raising steam conditions will benefit the process by increasing cycle efficiency and reducing specific emission concentrations: the first supercritical PFBC unit, of $350MW_e$ capacity, is under construction in Japan (Karita).

Integrated Gasification Combined Cycle (IGCC)

Power generation systems based on gasification of coal are considered to offer the potential for extremely low emissions. In IGCC plant, fuel-gas (ie, a gas containing carbon monoxide and hydrogen) derived from gasification of coal under pressure is burnt and expanded in a gas turbine to generate about two-thirds of the electricity. Hot exhaust gas from the gas turbine is used to generate steam which produces the rest of the electricity. Current built/operating IGCC systems offer efficiencies of around 43% (at local conditions) with very low emission levels (typically 25mg/Nm^3 of SO_2, 150mg/Nm^3 of NO_x and 5mg/Nm^3 of particulates). Further developments are expected to result in efficiencies in excess of 50% by early in the next century. Currently, a number of coal-based IGCC units are being demonstrated worldwide, ie, Buggenum (The Netherlands) - 250MW$_e$, Polk (USA) - 250MW$_e$ and Puertollano (Spain) - 320MW$_e$. The 260MW$_e$ Wabash River IGCC plant in the USA, though supported by the US Clean Coal Technology Demonstration Program, is now described as being in commercial operation. Several further potential coal-based IGCC units are currently under consideration in countries such as Germany (Goldenberg-Werk), the USA, the UK (Kellingley) and Japan. A more detailed review of the status of gasification technologies for power generation has recently been published (ref. 15).

Hybrid cycles

Systems which combine features of both coal gasification and combustion are commonly referred to as hybrid cycles. Hybrid cycles have been under development in the USA, Germany and the UK. A 107MW$_e$ demonstration plant has been constructed at Piñon Pine in the USA and is currently undergoing commissioning. The High Temperature Winkler (HTW) process has been developed to the demonstration stage in Germany, though this development currently appears to have been put on hold. In the UK, work has progressed over recent years to develop the ABGC. The ABGC process uses a pressurised air- and steam-blown spouted fluidised bed gasifier and an atmospheric circulating fluidised bed combustor (CFBC) to provide, respectively, fuel-gas for a gas turbine and steam for a steam turbine. The gasifier converts part of the fuel (around 80%) to a low calorific value fuel-gas, whilst residual char is burnt as a single fuel, or in combination with another fuel, in the CFBC to raise steam. A schematic of the ABGC is shown in Figure B1. Various key component systems of the ABGC are currently at an advanced stage of development. The ABGC is expected to be ready for demonstration in the near future which could achieve an efficiency of around 45%. However, efficiencies >50% are thought to be possible in the long-term with further R&D activities to improve gas turbine and other component systems.

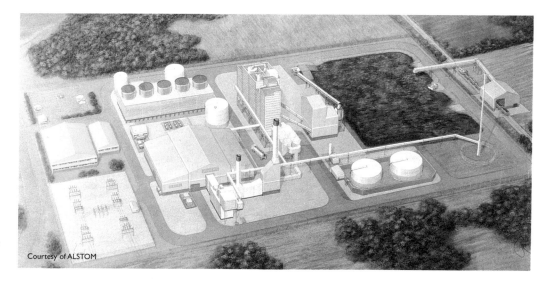

Artist's impression of an ABGC plant

Courtesy of ALSTOM

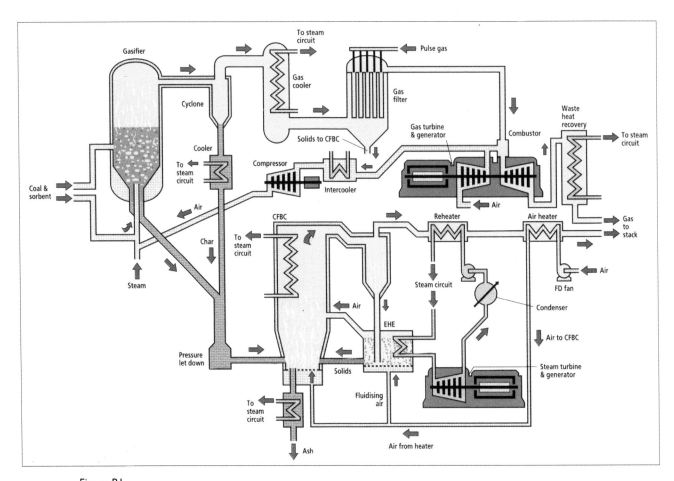

Figure B1.
A schematic of
the ABGC

Table B2 - Relative merits of pf vs advanced systems

Parameters	Conventional Combustion	Advanced Combustion		Gasification	Hybrid Cycle (gasification and combustion)
	Subcritical pf	Supercritical pf	PFBC	IGCC	ABGC
Maturity of technology	Completely proven and commercially available with guarantees	Substantially proven and commercial plant available with guarantees	Substantially proven and commercial plant available with guarantees	Mainly demonstration plant operational where coal is the fuel source	Still at R&D stage
Range of units available	All commercial sizes available (common unit size in the range 300-1000MW$_e$)	All commercial sizes available	Three sizes are available	250-300MW$_e$, currently limited by the size of large gas turbine units available	Demonstration plant proposed at around 90MW$_e$
Fuel flexibility	Burns a wide range of internationally traded coals	Burns a wide range of internationally traded coals	Will burn a wide range of internationally traded coals, as well as low grade coals efficiently; best suited for low ash coals	Should use a wide range of internationally traded coals, but not proven; Not really designed for low grade, high ash coals	Should use a wide range of internationally traded coals; designed to utilise low grade, high ash coals efficiently
Thermal efficiency (LHV)	Limited by steam conditions - around 41% with modern designs	At least 45% now possible and over 50% subject to successful materials development ie further R&D	Around 44% possible, some increases likely with further R&D and/or with supercritical steam cycle	Around 43% currently possible, but over 50% possible with advanced gas turbines and further R&D	Around 43% should be obtainable, but over 50% possible with advanced gas turbines and further R&D
Operational flexibility	Can operate at low load, but performance would be limited	Can operate at low load, but performance would be limited	Can operate at low load but performance would be limited	Realistically could only operate at base load	Design suggests would have reasonable performance at low load
Environmental performance	Good SO$_X$ and NO$_X$ reduction with FGD and low-NO$_X$ systems fitted; low efficiency means that CO$_2$ emissions high	Higher efficiency will reduce SO$_X$ and NO$_X$ emissions as well as CO$_2$	Good for SO$_X$ and NO$_X$ and reasonable for CO$_2$ due to relatively high efficiency, but solid waste may be difficult to dispose of	Excellent: inert slag, sulphur capture and low NO$_X$; high efficiency results in lower CO$_2$ emissions	Not proven, but should be as good as PFBC
Availability	Proven to be excellent	Proven to be good	Limited experience	Demonstration so far not satisfactory	Not yet demonstrated
Build time	Around 3 years	Around 3 years	Around 3 years	Around 4-5 years	3-4 years?

Comparison of various coal-based power generation systems

The main features of various coal-based power generation systems that are currently available or at an advanced stage of development are compared in Table B2. The cost of plant is notoriously difficult to establish because of the high number of variables involved and therefore is not included in Table B2. Where plant is to be constructed, on-site or remote fabrication of components, precisely what the cost includes, separation of cost and price, time to construct, and emissions targets are each examples of contributions to the whole which make costs virtually impossible to disentangle, and comparing costs extremely difficult. Recently, IEA Coal Research - The Clean Coal Centre, which is based in the UK, in collaboration with Sydkraft Konsult (Denmark) and the US Department of Energy, carried out a study (ref. 16) to model the competitiveness of various coal-based power generation systems. This was an attempt to disentangle costs by having a fairly rigid set of assumptions which apply to each plant type considered. All inputs to the model have been carefully selected such that there are a common set of "base assumptions" on matters ranging from costs of finance to steam conditions to coal type and price. The outputs allow a range of clean coal technologies to be compared. Though the main results from the study were presented in absolute terms, it was felt more appropriate for this report that they be presented as relative values, as shown in Table B3.

Table B3 - Efficiency and cost of advanced systems

Model outputs	Subcritical pf	Supercritical pf	Ultrasupercritical pf	IGCC	PFBC
Efficiency % (LHV basis at ISO conditions)	1	1.05	1.13	1.13	1.10
Total capital cost/kW$_e$	1	1	1.04	1.28	1.12

Annex C

Technical Objectives and Targets Established for the Programme of Work Outlined in Energy Paper 63

Technical and related policy objectives

Summarised below is a report on the extent to which the past programme of work outlined in Energy Paper 63 met its technical, administrative and policy objectives. The individual objectives and targets formed a key part of the agreed ROAME Statement or strategy for this programme (see Glossary for full definition of ROAME which stands for Rationale, Objectives, Appraisal, Monitoring and Evaluation). A similar set of objectives will be prepared for the new programme and progress on achieving them will be summarised in the published annual reports.

> To ensure that the strategic R&D work currently being undertaken by both the Coal Research Establishment (CRE) and the Technical Services and Research Executive (TSRE) are completed, and that satisfactory and appropriate technology transfer of the results is undertaken by the end of the programme.

All the strategic R&D work on cleaner coal technologies undertaken by CRE, TSRE and their successors was completed within the ROAME period. All the advanced power generation work undertaken by the successor to CRE - British Coal's Coal Technology Development Division (CTDD) - was completed, largely under the supervision of the Clean Coal Power Generation Group (CCPGG). This industry-led group established a technology transfer plan for the work, which is currently being pursued. The TSRE work was overseen by representatives from the mining industry and the Health and Safety Executive.

> In collaboration with the steps being undertaken by the Coal Privatisation Unit, ensure that CRE and TSRE (research division) become self-sustaining by the end of the programme.

As indicated above, all the strategic cleaner coal technology R&D is now under the leadership of industry. Coal Privatisation decisions led to the successful privatisation of both CRE and TSRE, whilst CTDD closed following the completion of its strategic advanced power generation contracts at the end of December 1997.

> To have initiated, in collaboration with the industry-led consortium, all the necessary research activity (in excess of 40 projects) for taking forward the development work for advanced power generation in which the UK has a technological lead (by mid-1994).

CCPGG members identified and managed a programme of R&D necessary to develop both the major individual components comprising the Air Blown Gasification Cycle (ABGC) and the ABGC technology itself to the stage where a prototype integrated plant could be specified. The Agreement under which the CCPGG members collaborated expired at the end of December 1997. The work programme was completed and the objectives of the CCPGG met. Results were encouraging and the ABGC technology is currently being taken forward by UK industry (ALSTOM, Mitsui Babcock Energy Ltd and ScottishPower).

To have completed an evaluation and assessment of the opportunities for utilising UK coals for alternative uses and initiated appropriate research (in excess of ten projects). This includes completion of the Point of Ayr coal liquefaction project (March 1995).

Fourteen collaborative R&D projects were initiated to look at alternative uses for UK coals. These projects, supported by a number of additional university-based research projects and three scoping studies, have enabled an evaluation and assessment of opportunities to be made. The Point of Ayr coal liquefaction project was completed and reports on the project issued. A Technology Status Report on liquefaction technology is being prepared for the IEA by the DTI to further promote the technology.

To identify novel coal extraction and coal preparation concepts and to determine by the end of 1995/96, via at least five projects, whether they merit further development (this includes completion of the EC Underground Coal Gasification Project and an appraisal of whether further work merits consideration).

Seventeen collaborative R&D projects, supported by a number of university-based research projects, have been undertaken in these technology areas. To help identify priorities for future R&D, three scoping studies have been performed. All site work for the Underground Coal Gasification Project is now complete and the project has entered its final appraisal and reporting phase. Further work in this area is currently under consideration in collaboration with the Coal Authority.

Administration and management

To achieve 75% of projects completed to time and budget.

Of the completed contracts in the programme, 64% have been completed without time extensions and 92% have been completed within budget. Overall, 61% have been completed to time and budget. Time extensions have mostly been of short duration and usually required in order to obtain an acceptable final report; often, delays have arisen, for example, due to the different reporting requirements of other funding bodies used for collaborative projects. If contracts with time extensions of less than three months are excluded, the respective percentages are 78%, 92% and 75%.

To achieve 75% of the objectives set for projects within the programme.

The programme has achieved this. Of the projects which have been evaluated by the programme's Advisory Committee on Coal Research (ACCR), between 80% and 90% of identified objectives have been achieved.

To secure positive exploitation (through patents, licensing or industrial use of the results) from at least 20% of the projects during the programme period, and 40% within five years of the end of the programme.

During the programme period, a technology transfer and exports strategy was developed and implemented. Part of this strategy was to prepare technology transfer and exploitation plans for each project within the programme, in consultation with the contractors. This approach has ensured that exploitation opportunities have been optimised and that the targets identified for the ROAME Statement period, and beyond, would be met. This is an ongoing exercise, and the new programme will focus on both promoting the results of completed projects from this programme and those arising from the new programme.

To disseminate the results of the programme through the publication of Project Profiles, Summaries, Reports and other information dissemination activities, eg programme newsletters and annual reports.

As part of the programme's technology transfer and exports strategy, project-specific literature (Project Profiles, Project Summaries and Final Reports) plus literature of a more programme-wide nature (UK Capability Brochures, Technology Status Reports, Case Studies, Highlights Brochures and Newsletters) have been produced. These publications have been widely distributed using a database containing some 600 addresses of relevant names/ organisations. Over 520 items of literature have been published since April 1990 and over 435 items were published within the period of the ROAME Statement.

To obtain at least 80% of the funding necessary to meet the objectives of the programme over its lifetime from external sources.

The DTI's contribution to the total portfolio of R&D is £52.6 million against a total value of £275 million; this represents a 19.1% contribution. Hence, over 80% of the funding has been met from external sources.

To secure participation in the programme of the 40 key UK companies with an interest in clean coal technologies (these companies account for the majority of commercial activity related to such technology).

Sixty-four companies have had close involvement in R&D projects supported by the Programme. Throughout this period, a very substantial number of companies and organisations have been involved indirectly via sub-contracts and the like. Furthermore, over 200 additional companies have been involved in the programme through participation in its technology transfer and exports activities, for example, the China and India Trade Missions of 1996 and 1997, and the development of the Export Directory and resulting database.

To have encouraged at least three further collaborations involving UK industry with the US DOE's clean coal technology programmes.

In addition to collaborations via IEA Programmes, three projects and two technology workshops have been initiated involving UK industry with the US DOE's programmes. A number of other potential collaborations have been proposed which will be pursued under the new programme.

To have secured at least "juste retour" for the UK in the Framework Programme and ECSC Technical Coal Research Programme with respect to UK projects for clean coal technology.

For the THERMIE 1994 and 1995 rounds, the UK obtained more than juste retour for UK-led projects. For example, in the 1994 round, some 34% of the solid fuel THERMIE budget was secured for two UK-based projects (Point of Ayr and Longannet) worth £6.8 million. In the 1995 round, some 16.7 % of the THERMIE budget went to UK-led projects worth some £5 million. Following a very limited number of UK submissions to the 1996 THERMIE round, projects with UK participation, including the UK-led proposal to develop further the ABGC, were successful in the 1997 THERMIE round. Over the past few years the UK has consistently been successful is obtaining 30% or more of the ECSC budget for coal utilisation technologies and a similar percentage for mining-related projects.

To have initiated at least 30 new collaborative projects with the Science and Engineering Research Council (SERC).

Thirty-seven projects were enlisted under the terms of the Joint-Funding Agreement between the DTI and the SERC (now the Engineering and Physical Sciences Research Council (EPSRC)). A new collaborative initiative with EPSRC will also form part of the new programme.

To further improve the co-ordination of the UK coal science activity in universities and industry such that all the coal science projects have a degree of industrial involvement (ie, a technical and/or financial contribution) by 1995.

The Joint-Funding Agreements with EPSRC and the British Coal Utilisation Research Association (BCURA) have facilitated considerable co-ordination with other DTI-funded collaborative projects. In addition, the programme has worked closely with the Coal Research Forum in the exchange of information and ideas. This has helped to prioritise and steer proposals coming to both EPSRC and BCURA. All coal science projects supported directly by the DTI (ie, not via the Joint-Funding Agreements) had industrial involvement.

To increase the participation of small and medium-sized enterprises (SMEs) in the programme from the present ten to 30 by the end of the five year programme.

Of the 47 UK companies directly involved in the programme's R&D activities, at least 18 were SMEs. However, many more SMEs have had indirect involvement either as sub-contractors or as equipment/component suppliers. For example, well in excess of 100 SMEs were sub-contracted to the portfolio of projects overseen by the CCPGG. Implementation of the technology transfer and exports strategy also involved a number of SMEs. Some seven SMEs participated in the cleaner coal technology trade missions to China and India of 1996 and 1997, respectively, and over 65 further SMEs participated in the programme through inclusion in the Export Directory promoting their expertise and equipment.

Annex D

The UK Opportunities for Coal Bed Methane

Introduction   This Annex briefly reviews the extraction of methane from UK coal beds as a resource in its own right, and not as a mining hazard, emission or by-product. It identifies the potential of coal bed methane (CBM) to contribute to the UK's future energy supply if the not inconsiderable technical and economic barriers can be reduced over the next few years. A set of goals has been identified which, if they can be reached, could enable the UK to exploit its CBM resource. A report giving a detailed account of CBM technology, worldwide resources and reserves is available from IEA Coal Research - The Clean Coal Centre (ref. 17). The DTI is a member of the Executive Committee which oversees the work of IEA Coal Research, with financial contributions to its work also coming from UK industry.

Background   Virtually all coals contain some methane as the result of the original coalification process. As a general rule the methane content of coal increases with depth and with coal rank. Thus hard coals (anthracites and bituminous coals) have comparatively high levels, while brown coal and lignite have comparatively low levels. Part of this methane is released when the pore pressure of the coal is reduced or when the coal is de-stressed or fractured. The last two are inevitable when the coal is mined.

Methane is a flammable gas and forms an explosive mixture when mixed with air at concentrations between about 5% and 15%. Miners have long recognised its potential hazard and have used ventilation, or other methods, to keep the methane concentration, in the body of the mine air, within safe limits. One of the many options to reduce these emissions is to drill holes from the surface and to use these to pre-drain part of the methane. This then led to the concept of using this technique to abstract the methane, for use as a source of energy, independently of any mining operation. The gas produced is generally referred to as "coal bed methane" and this term is used in this review.

The gas obtained in this way is comparable to natural gas and can normally be mixed with pipeline-grade natural gas with only minimal treatment. While it is conventionally referred to as "methane", it generally contains some non-organic impurities (such as nitrogen or carbon dioxide), plus small amounts of higher hydrocarbons (such as ethane).

Commercial CBM production started in the USA in 1978 and that country now has over 6,000 wells in operation, most of them in two specific coal basins. The most important of these is the San Juan Basin in Colorado. This produced $16 \times 10^9 m^3$ of gas from 2,612 wells in 1993. The other is the Black Warrior Basin in Alabama, which produced $3 \times 10^9 m^3$ of gas from 2,884 wells in the same year. It should be noted that this means that a typical San Juan well produced at a rate over six times that of a typical Black Warrior one. There were also considerable differences between wells in the same basin, depending on their location and the method of drilling and fracturing.

The commercial development of CBM in the USA has been aided by the presence of large and very suitable coal basins, a fully-integrated natural gas pipeline system, a major R&D capability, and a favourable tax regime.

It must be emphasised that the quantity of CBM that can be extracted depends on the properties of the coal and the drilling density, but the energy content of the gas will not generally exceed 1% of the total energy content of the host coal. In other words CBM is a way of obtaining some energy in a readily marketable form, but it is not equivalent to actually mining that coal. Nevertheless it is a useful energy resource, given that known coal reserves are an order of magnitude greater than known gas reserves. Also it is a means of obtaining some energy from coal seams that are not suitable for conventional mining.

An overview of the main coal basins in the UK and their potential for CBM is presented in Table D1, at the end of this Annex. As indicated in the table, the topography of the various CBM prospects in the UK varies considerably. This would influence both well-site costs and the ease of obtaining local authority planning consent. While most prospects lie beneath farmland, there are others near major conurbations or adjacent to estuaries. The South Wales coalfield presents some of the more difficult terrain with much of the coal being beneath steep and forested hills.

Coal as a methane reservoir

Much of the methane produced during coalification has dissipated over geological time; however, the quantities which remain typically range from a trace to $25m^3/t$. This remaining methane is stored in a fundamentally different way from the methane in a more normal sandstone reservoir. In these the gas is compressed within the void spaces within the rock matrix. Coal can store more gas than could be accounted for in this way.

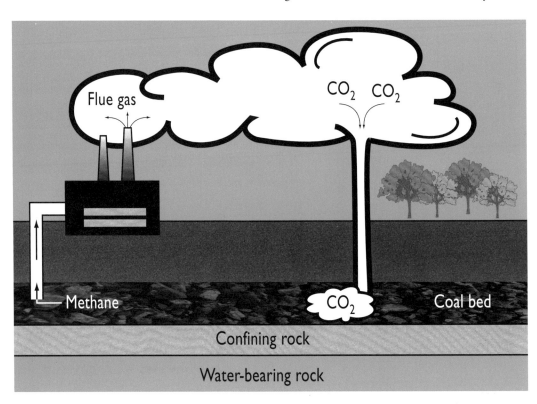

A schematic of the coal bed methane utilisation process

It is now believed that the main mechanism for methane retention in coal is physical adsorption, ie retention on the coal surface within the pore structure. It is therefore the area of the pore surface, rather than the pore volume, which is critical. While the methane capacity of coal depends on its adsorption characteristics, its ability to produce methane depends on its permeability. In general terms permeability is the ability of a rock to conduct fluid. It is measured by the rate at which a fluid of standard viscosity moves with time.

Permeability depends on the size and shape of the pores and the way that they are interconnected. Coal generally has a pattern of natural fractures called "cleat" which provides this interconnection. The in-situ permeability of a coal seam is dependent on the cleat. An increase in confining stress can result in cleat closure and a reduction in permeability; if the cleat contains minerals these can also reduce permeability.

In order for methane to flow out of a coal seam it is necessary to reduce the pressure in the seam. If the seam is water-saturated, then pumping out the water is one way of achieving this. The methane then desorbs from the micropores closest to the cleat. The rate of diffusion through solid coal is very low, so a well-developed cleat fracture system is important for commercial CBM extraction.

Production technology

The USA has the most experience of the commercial extraction of CBM. This section is therefore very heavily dependent on US experience. In the USA the normal method is to drill vertical holes from the surface. Originally these were cased to the top of the seam to be drained. The hole was then drilled through the seam, leaving a sump beneath, and this portion was left "openhole". Current practice is to run the casing through the seam and then to use small explosive charges to make slots or perforations in the casing at seam level. Generally this has resulted in higher gas productions than from the openhole method. There are, however, exceptions. A variant of the openhole technique has been used effectively in parts of the San Juan Basin.

Whatever drilling method is used, it is generally necessary to "stimulate" or enhance the permeability of the coal in some way. The normal method is by "hydraulic fracturing". This is a technique borrowed from the oil industry, where it is used to enhance reservoir permeability. Packers are located above and below the section to be fractured so that a high fluid pressure can be applied to the seam. The fractures are usually initiated by pumping in a low-viscosity fluid at pressures of around 350bar, with the main slurry rate being pumped at around 200bar. These are then widened by pumping in a higher-viscosity fluid containing a granular "propping" agent. The proppant prevents the fractures closing when the pressure is released. The fracture, which may be over 10mm wide and several hundred metres long, provides a conductive path to the well bore. In CBM wells nitrogen foam or water is generally used as the pumped fluid, with sand being added to act as the proppant.

In the case of multiple seams it is possible to perforate and fracture at each seam level. This would be useful in European coalfields, where multiple seams are the norm.

Another technique for possibly achieving better fractures is the openhole dynamic cavitation method, which has recently been developed in the San Juan Basin. This is based on stopping the casing above the coal seam and then drilling through and repeatedly injecting water-air mixtures at high rates and pressures to bring about controlled blow outs. The result is that the borehole enlarges to form a cavity and the stresses are lowered around it, leading nearby fractures to open and become more permeable. The critical reservoir conditions for this technique are still only partially understood, but appear to be low stress levels with good permeability, adequate seam thickness and fully gas-charged coals. It is still not clear why this gives better results in the San Juan Basin and it is so far the only area to give better results. The San Juan Basin is arguably a unique geological setting, and UK coals are far more comparable to the Black Warrior Basin geology. This technique would probably render the coal unworkable by underground mining methods due to cavitation and therefore should only take place where mining in unlikely.

US experience is that once the sand and debris has been cleaned up it is usually necessary to dewater the coal bed. This is because most of their wells are in seams which are water-saturated. Abstracting water from the cleat fractures reduces the pressure so that the methane begins to desorb from the coal's microporosity closest to the cleat. The well starts by producing water and then a mixture of water and methane in a two-phase flow. Water abstraction is normally by sucker-rod-pumps ("nodding donkeys") or gas-fired engines. Submersible pumps could be used, but experience with these to-date has not been encouraging.

However, not all coal seams are water saturated. Where this is not the case it is likely to make CBM abstraction more difficult, irrespective of the generally low permeability of UK coals. However, coalfields have aquifers and it is likely that fracturing the coal seams could result in fractures extending to the aquifers with resultant inflows of water.

The criteria for well spacing for maximum CBM recovery are different from those in conventional gas reservoirs. In conventional reservoirs, wells that are spaced too close together tend to "compete" for gas located in the overlapping areas. In CBM wells closer spacing may be beneficial as a denser pattern will cause additional pressure reduction, and thus increase the desorption rate. However, pressure reduction can only be accomplished within bounded structures and this geological control will set well spacings.

Other CBM drilling options are to obtain access to the target seam from existing workings or from a specially excavated shaft. It is then possible to drill a series of holes running within the coal seam. If a shaft needs to be sunk then the costs involved generally rule out this option - that is compared with conventional vertical drilling. A development of the shaft concept would be to use directional drill techniques, where a hole is drilled from the surface, initially vertical, but then diverted to run in the coal seam. This is not considered an economic option at present, but it could become so in the future as directional drilling techniques are continually improving, leading to higher success rates and lower costs. By drilling a "fan" of holes from one location it could also considerably reduce the number of surface locations, which could have considerable environmental benefits, especially in a country such as the UK. This aspect is considered in more detail below.

The injection of an inert gas, such as carbon dioxide or nitrogen, into the methane-bearing strata could be used as a means of increasing methane emissions. This would occur because the gas injection would reduce the partial pressure of the methane. Some work has been done on this concept, but the economics have not been favourable, given the costs of isolating, transporting and compressing the gas. These economics could change in the case of carbon dioxide if there were a requirement to dispose of anthropological carbon dioxide, so as to reduce the effect that this gas has on global warming.

Environmental aspects

Commercial CBM extraction requires a large number of holes. One authority proposes 125 wells over an area of 40km² as the minimum for a commercial operation. While this might be acceptable in the less populated parts of the USA, particularly in areas which are accustomed to oil or gas extraction, the impact of this number of boreholes and off-take points in rural UK should not be underestimated. This is not to say that the problem could not be solved, rather that it would have to be approached cautiously.

It has been estimated that a UK production site might require an area of 0.25ha (say 50m x 50m); this area includes provision for visual screening by trees, shrubs or earth mounds. The individual areas would have to be interconnected by piping, to handle the gas produced and to dispose of the water pumped out. This piping would probably have to be buried for visual reasons and to allow normal rural activities to continue.

An alternative to such a pipeline system could be the use of small generator sets taking gas from a small group of boreholes. Similar technology is currently used for utilising the gas produced from landfill sites.

Water quantities and qualities can vary greatly, even in the same coal basin. In some cases the pH and the total dissolved solids may be such that the water can be discharged to a local watercourse, but it would be wiser to assume that some sort of treatment will be necessary. The main factors which may require water treatment are salinity (generally measured as total dissolved solids) and the possible toxic or ecological effects of certain inorganic irons and trace organic substances. Discharge after aeration and setting is likely to be sufficient, although limestone or other chemicals may need to be added to control the pH.

It is possible to reinject all or some of the water back into the coal strata, provided precautions are taken to ensure that no aquifers, being used for water extraction, are contaminated.

Advance treatment processes are possible, but the costs involved are likely to be high. It is therefore reasonable to assume that the quality and quantity of water likely to be produced will be a key item in evaluating the overall economics of a specific resource.

Economics

Available cost data is very limited, partly from commercial confidentiality and partly because it varies so much from basin to basin. Although UK drilling costs are not significantly different to US figures, what does dramatically increase well costs are the ancillary services such as stimulating and cementing. There are also likely to be significant waste water disposal costs.

UK experience in CBM

Under the Petroleum [Production] Act 1934, oil and natural gas in the strata underlying the UK is the property of the Crown. The Coal Industry Act 1994, which provided for the privatisation of the British Coal Corporation (BCC), confirmed that CBM is also vested in the Crown. Companies are licensed by the DTI to explore for, and abstract, oil and gas including CBM. Where these access coal seams, agreement is needed from the Coal Authority as owner of virtually all coal in the UK. Such agreements need to recognise the existing rights of others to work coal.

One of the problems, prior to this, had been that BCC had been seeking substantial payments for CBM licences, together with free access to data generated and a large degree of control over the operations.

Section 3 (5) of the Coal Industry Act imposes on the Coal Authority a duty, in the exercise of its powers and duties, "to have regard to the desirability of the exploitation, so far as is economically viable, of coal bed methane in Great Britain". On the basis of this the Coal Authority has agreed to provide access to the ex-BCC geological database on a commercial but inexpensive basis.

Superficially, CBM exploration activity in the UK looks promising. Several wells have been drilled but many encountered problems with drilling techniques. Interest continues and several companies plan to drill further wells. The first well was drilled in 1992 by Evergreen Resources (UK) Ltd at Sealand near Chester, and they have returned to the area to conduct further studies. Wells have also been drilled at Rhuddlan in north Wales and Margam Forest in south Wales. Coal Bed Methane Ltd are also currently developing the Airth-Arns Farm project in the Midland Valley in Scotland. Much of the current interest is in abstracting gas from mined-out areas - gob gas in US terminology. Companies going along this route include: Octagon (UK) Ltd, which has a licence at Whitehaven in Cumbria; UK Gas Ltd, with an area in south Wales; and Coalgas (UK) Ltd, with a number of blocks south of Doncaster. In several of these cases it will be possible to take gas from the existing mine vents, without further drilling work.

One of the environmental problems that will be encountered as the UK moves to commercial CBM production will be the individual well-head connection areas and the piping necessary to connect these to the end users. These problems could be reduced by reducing the density of collection points by the use of directional drilling. This approach has not generally been used in the USA due to the higher costs of directional drilling. It may, however, be the only acceptable way in the UK, given that the density of in-seam penetrations is likely to have to be similar to, or greater than, that used in the USA because of the lower permeability of UK coals.

Relative costs of directional drilling are however decreasing as the oil and gas industry gains greater experience in its use. Directional drilling is likely to require a rethink of CBM technology. For example, one option might be to drill diverted holes in-seam, perpendicular to the cleat (ie to the direction of greatest permeability); and then to hydrofrac at a series of points within the seam. The use of diverted holes would require the use of submersible pumps - rather than the traditional "nodding donkey" - for dewatering.

Wider benefits of exploiting CBM

Enhanced CBM Recovery and Climate Change

The use of some form of enhanced gas-recovery could improve both production rates and the extraction percentage of the in-situ resource. One option is to inject another gas, such as carbon dioxide (CO_2) to displace the methane. CO_2 injection is currently being used successfully in New Mexico. The injected CO_2 replaces the methane held in the micropore structure of the coal matrix and remains in the ground after the completion of methane production. Further development is required if this technology is to be applied in geological conditions that are present in the UK. Unlike conventional CBM recovery, which requires depletion of reservoir pressure and generally recovers around 50% of gas in place, enhanced CBM allows maintenance of reservoir pressure. Simulation and early demonstration projects indicate that the technology is capable of recovering 90% or more of methane in place, while accelerating methane recovery. As well as the technical problems, there are the cost implications of providing the CO_2. A further consideration would be the need to avoid areas of past, present and future coal mining activities resulting in uncontrolled emissions.

The economics may change, however, if credit can be taken for the removal of CO_2 from the atmosphere. The technology could be employed to sequester large volumes of CO_2 in deep coal seam reservoirs, thereby reducing emissions of this greenhouse gas. Any method which would act as a "sink" for CO_2 would therefore have substantial environmental benefits. Experimentally measured absorption isotherms for coal suggest that two molecules of CO_2 can replace one of methane. This means that the "sink" could potentially absorb more CO_2 than that generated by the combustion of the methane (one molecule of methane, on combustion, produces one molecule of CO_2). The technology may also help to commercialise CBM resources that have low permeability and undersaturation - the position in the UK. For example, maintaining reservoir pressure by injecting CO_2 may keep coal cleats open and thus maintain permeability.

The DTI is participating in a major project to develop CO_2 injection technology in Canada in collaboration with Canadian and US Government organisations, major oil companies, power utilities and gas supply companies. The project is being undertaken under the auspices of the IEA's Greenhouse Gas R&D Programme Agreement to which the DTI is a signatory. This Agreement is one of the IEA's principal focuses for work on the sequestration of CO_2 and a number of studies have been undertaken on the technical aspects of CBM and the broad economics associated with the technology.

Potential for Increasing the Life of North Sea Gas Reserves

The successful application of CBM technology on the UK mainland could also have an important spin-off in extending the life of North Sea natural gas fields. For CBM to be economic on the UK mainland, more innovative drilling and production methods will need to be developed which may have offshore application. The big offshore gas fields are not suited to CBM technology as they have had big investment in compression and bottom hole pressures are lower than those obtainable by CBM pumping. However, CBM technology may have an important niche market in many of the smaller fields, notably those water-affected gas fields not linked to a compression infrastructure.

CBM techniques may offer important, low-cost technology specifically geared to fractured, tight and difficult reservoirs. If they can be developed successfully for CBM application onshore, low-cost stimulation and production technologies could be applied offshore and reduce well costs and operational expenditure. In the longer-term, as pressures decrease offshore, the safety requirements could be relaxed, allowing more economic developments using CBM know-how.

The way forward for the UK   There are three areas of interest to the UK:

- the development of its indigenous CBM reserves;

- the opportunity for UK firms to exploit their experience overseas.;

- the contribution CBM technology may make to increasing the life of North Sea gas reserves.

The first of these is going to require some rethinking of the methods which, while they have worked in the USA, have not been so successful in the UK. Areas which may need addressing include:

- the importance of permeability, and ways of enhancing this;

- obtaining a better knowledge of the properties of UK coals, in so far as they affect CBM emission;

- as the UK source-seams will be those which have not already been exploited by underground mining, this probably means operating at considerably greater depth than is normal in the USA;

- as the fact that many seams are not water-saturated means that de-watering is not a method of inducing gas emission, other methods need to be found - the concept of using another gas, such as carbon dioxide or nitrogen, might be one such option;

- the concept of underground disposal of carbon dioxide has environmental benefits, but the compression and transport problems should not be underestimated.

As far as exporting UK technology is concerned, the key geographical areas of interest should include China, India and Eastern Europe (in particular Russia, Poland, Ukraine and Kazakhstan). Both China and India have coal reserves which considerably exceed their oil and (natural) gas reserves. They both have increasing primary energy requirements, as the standard of living of their populations rises. CBM is therefore a useful, and potentially clean, source of energy for them. Russia has plenty of natural gas, but such reserves have a finite life. Another point that must be borne in mind is the immense size of these three countries and their comparatively unsophisticated transport systems. This means that there will for the foreseeable future be certain areas where certain fuels have an advantage.

Poland, Ukraine and Kazakhstan all have large coal reserves, but only very limited oil and gas. They currently import gas from Russia, but an indigenous source would have obvious balance of payments benefits. In the Ukraine and Poland conventional underground mining is getting progressively more difficult as the more accessible seams become exhausted. CBM would be one way of obtaining some energy from deep and inaccessible seams.

It must be recognised that developments in all these countries are likely to require external finance. This could be in the form of loans from international lending agencies (such as the World Bank), from EC sources or from individual Governments. Another option would be the granting of exploration and extraction licences to western companies. This has been done in Poland already, although the results, to date, have been negative.

While Australia and Canada have large CBM resources it is most likely that they will wish to develop their own technologies. The same argument applies, to a lesser extent, to South Africa. These three countries would therefore seem to offer limited opportunities for UK technology; although there could be opportunities for the exchange of information and technologies. The IEA Agreement structure would seem the most appropriate route to encourage such an exchange. The DTI will be examining the scope for further collaboration under the auspices of the IEA to encourage and promote collaborative initiatives such as the Canadian CO_2 sequestration project.

The extent to which these areas can be addressed will depend in the first instance on the success of developing the technology to a point where commercial exploitation of CBM resources is achieved.

Next steps   *Research and Development Issues*

The DTI has commissioned Wardell Armstrong and British Geological Survey to examine what R&D may be needed to encourage wider exploitation of the UK's CBM resource. The DTI has also identified six technical and economic goals for the programme if CBM is to have any realistic opportunity to have widespread potential in the UK. The review of priorities for R&D should enable a portfolio of projects to be initiated to enable these goals to be met. These can be summarised as follows:

- Better mechanical methods of enhancing the permeability of UK coals. *The lower permeability of UK coals, and indeed coals in general, when compared to those of the San Juan and Black Warrior Basins in the USA seems to be one of the main problems in achieving commercial CBM extraction.*

- Obtain reliable estimates of the costs of CBM extraction and, in particular, identify significant cost components. *Initial data from the USA suggests significant waste water disposal cost. Should the proposed research confirm this result, then technological advances and cost efficiencies in this area must become a priority if CBM extraction is to become commercially viable.*

- Examine and cost two options for enhancing CBM release. Examples include carbon dioxide and nitrogen injection. *These technologies are seen as being distinct from "mechanical" fracturing methods, although they might be combined in practice - this goal is being addressed, at least initially, through the UK's participation in the Canadian CO_2 injection project.*

- Identify the other key CBM release parameters. *There is more to CBM extraction than just strata permeability. A better understanding of the mechanics of the system is required.*

- Determine the current UK reserves of CBM and consider ways that these could be increased. *All that exists at the moment is an estimated resource of $2x10^{12}m^3$* (ref. 17).

- Achieve commercial CBM extraction in at least one coalfield area, preferably in more than one location in that area. *The UK is currently using US technology, or at least a modification of it. This may not be the answer; it may be necessary to develop more innovative techniques or go back to first principles.*

- Identify the break-even conditions which would have to be achieved if CBM is to compete with North Sea gas.

Regulation and Licensing Issues

The Government is aware of concerns that the present hydrocarbon licensing system in the UK does not provide an appropriate mechanism to regulate the activities of companies involved in the exploration for, and exploitation of, CBM because it is based on the different, and perhaps more onerous, requirements of conventional oil and gas projects. In response to these concerns, the DTI has been examining what legislative changes may be introduced to further encourage CBM exploration and development. However, any proposals for a new licence regime will be subject to consultation with industry.

All CBM potential in the UK lies within carboniferous coalfields. These are well defined and generally well explored. Most have been mined at several horizons over wide areas, but there are other areas which are unmined. In particular there are significant and intact successions remaining at depth. The main coalfields are:

Table D1 - CBM potential of different UK coalfields

Scotland (Midland Valley)

This is a graben (rift system) which contains the main Scottish coalfield. There is a key area between Falkirk and the northern Boundary, with numerous unworked seams at depth, which could have CBM potential. A similar situation is found near the east Fife coast, but the main basin there lies offshore.

Canonbie and Cumberland

This is a southwest-northeast trending basin which straddles the England-Scotland border. The west Cumberland portion has largely been mined out. The Canonbie area has only been explored by a few deep boreholes, but seismic reflection data suggests that a concealed coalfield extend farther to the southwest below the Solway estuary, to connect in the subsurface with the west Cumbria area.

Northeast England

This comprises the Northumberland and Durham coalfields, the latter overlying a structural "high" (Alston Block). Most of the area is mined out and the coal gas contents are generally low. There is, therefore, only likely to be limited CBM interest.

The Pennine Basin

The Pennine Basin is a large carboniferous structure, some 200km in diameter, incorporating all the main coalfields of north-central England together with north Wales. As in the Scottish Midland valley, coal concentrations vary according to location, but on more regional scales. Individual coalbeds thicken towards the basin centre, while thick coal beds are also found around the basin margins. The locations of most interest for CBM are likely to be in the intermediate areas (between the basin centre and the margins), in which there is a significant uneroded coal succession at depths sufficient for gas generation and retention. North Staffordshire, Lancashire and parts of north Wales best fulfil these requirements and generally have a higher retained gas content than Nottinghamshire and Yorkshire. The western fields also have a different structure, with large throw faults which compartmentalise the ground into blocks, many of which remain unmined at depth.

Warwickshire and Oxfordshire

These coalfields mainly lie across a geological "high" rather than within a basin. Their gas contents are generally low. The Oxfordshire coals have never been mined.

South Wales and Southern England

There is a range of coal ranks, especially in south Wales where there are large areas of anthracite. Much of the western third of the coalfield, including the anthracite area, is unworked as the depths along the main west-east synclinal axis are too deep for conventional mining.

The geology of the lower coals in the Kent and structurally complex Somerset coalfields are the least well known, so their gas evolution and retention properties may be quite dissimilar to the previously mined coals. The Kent coals may be water-saturated, which could help CBM release.

Annex E

The UK Opportunities for Underground Coal Gasification

Introduction　　This Annex briefly reviews underground coal gasification technology (UCG) and identifies its potential to contribute to the UK's future energy supply if the not inconsiderable technical and economic barriers can be reduced over the next few years. A set of goals have been identified which, if they can be reached over the next five years or so, could enable the UK to exploit UCG technology, at home and overseas in the 21st century.

Background　　A method of obtaining at least some of the energy from coal, without going through the physical mining process, has obvious attractions. Underground coal mining, even with modern mining machinery, is an arduous and potentially dangerous operation, while open cast (surface) mining can give rise to environmental objections which are difficult to reconcile with other land use activities. UCG, like coal bed methane, is an option, but it too may give rise to environmental problems that would need to be addressed.

At its simplest UCG involves passing oxygen, with the possible addition of water, through a pre-heated underground bed of coal. The product is a gas containing methane, hydrogen and carbon monoxide. The chemistry involved is comparable to the processes traditionally used to produce towns-gas from coal, or those used in more modern coal gasification processes, although there are a number of detailed differences. The resultant gas also has a calorific value close to gas derived from coal gasification technologies developed for power application.

The concept is not new; it was operated on a commercial scale in Russia in the 1930s and a range of trials has been carried out in the USA and Europe. One of the early problems was in achieving an initial underground "circuit"; in some cases this involved the manual sinking of shafts and the construction of underground galleries - when a key objective was to avoid the need for men to work underground. Modern directional drilling techniques, developed by the oil and gas industry, have solved this problem and this aspect is considered in more detail below.

Most of the early work was carried out at shallow depths because this minimised the costs of the experiments and because the countries concerned had suitable coals at these depths. However, one of the potential advantages of UCG is that it could be used to abstract energy from seams too deep for conventional mining. In fact there are positive advantages in working at depth. It is possible to operate the reactor at a higher pressure - the safe pressure is basically limited to the hydrostatic pressure; this encourages the methane synthesis reaction and increases the calorific value of the product gas.

It is this aspect, the ability to operate at depth, which is of particular interest as far as the UK is concerned. While most of the UK shallower coal seams have been mined out, there are still large resources at depths greater than 1000m. This depth is generally regarded as the "cut off point" for conventional underground coal mining. Deeper than this the increasing virgin strata temperature, due to the geothermal gradient, makes it increasingly difficult to achieve acceptable working conditions. Also the greater strata pressures place constraints on mining methods. These are technical problems and can potentially be solved, but only at increased costs of production. However, anything which increases costs is not an option for the UK coal mining industry, which is having to reduce costs to remain competitive with imported coal.

Similar circumstances apply in a number of other Western European countries. Belgium and The Netherlands both ceased coal mining some years ago, having exhausted all their accessible coal reserves, and France, Germany and Spain only continue because their industries are subsidised in various ways.

There may also be some potential to gasify seams in old mining areas or seams considered unmineable using current technology at depths less than 1000m.

Underground Gasification Europe

It was against this background that the Underground Gasification Europe (UGE) project was established to carry out a field trial of UCG in Spain. The participants in this £14 million project were Spanish, Belgian and UK Government organisations, with additional funding being provided through the EC's THERMIE Programme. UGE is a "European Economic Interest Grouping", ie it is a legal entity established to carry out the trial, rather than a consortium of the various participants. The UK financial input of some £1.7 million was from the DTI, as part of its Cleaner Coal Technology Programme.

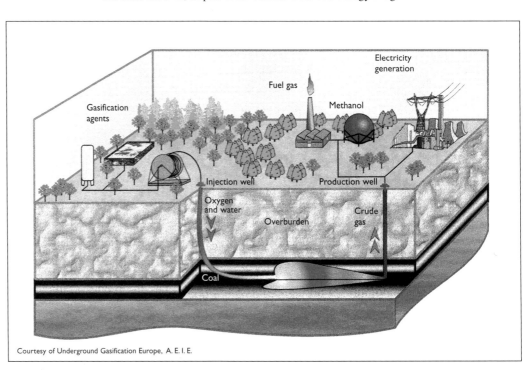

A schematic of an underground coal gasification system

Courtesy of Underground Gasification Europe, A. E. I. E.

The site chosen was near the town of Alcorisa in Teruel where there were two adjacent seams at a depth of between 500m and 600m and dipping at about 30°. The coal is sub-bituminous on the International classification; the Spanish refer to it as "black lignite". Obviously the site selected had to be remote from any operating mines. For economic reasons it also had to be in a block of coal which was not required for conventional mining at a later date.

The overall objective of the trial was to show that it was possible to gasify a European coal at a depth of between 500m and 600m and to produce a good-quality gas. While this depth was shallower than the preferred depth for UCG exploitation in the UK, it was considered to be a significant increase on most previous work and that techniques that were proved at this depth would also be applicable to greater depths.

Among the technical problems that had to be solved were the ability to drill deviated boreholes and the demonstration of the use of the Controlled Retraction Injection Point (CRIP) technique so as to maximise the amount of coal that could be gasified from a single set of boreholes.

A view of a drilling injection well in the Underground Gasification Europe project

Courtesy of A. J. K. Goode.

While some exploration drilling had been carried out in the general area - to assess the possibilities for conventional underground mining - the first stage of the project was to drill a further three exploration holes in the target area. These identified the depth, thickness and dip of the target seam. They also had a subsequent role as monitoring holes during the gasification phase. Based on this geological data the problem then became to drill a deviated hole which would start vertically, but then be "turned" through 60° so as to run within the seam - dipping at 30° - for a target distance of 100m. While such directional drilling, using a "down hole motor", is common in the oil and gas industries, the degree of absolute precision required - to remain within a coal seam about 2m thick - was unusual. One of the problems was that, while "measurement while drilling" (MWD) techniques were used, the equipment had, necessarily, to be mounted some distance behind the cutting head. It was therefore measuring where the cutting head had been, rather than where it was. Nevertheless a distance of about 90m, either in, or close to, the coal was achieved. This is an aspect which requires further development as commercial UCG would probably require the ability both to stay in seam for up to 500m and the ability to do this consistently. This deviated hole was to form the injection well for the trial.

The next requirement was to drill a "vertical" product well that would intersect - or pass close to - the deviated well, so as to form an underground "circuit". In practice this well was also deviated to a small extent as it neared the injection well. In fact the wells met within 1m and this was found to be adequate given the natural permeability of the coal.

On-surface facilities included, on the injection side, cryogenic tanks containing oxygen (for the gasification reaction) and nitrogen (for safety and other purposes) and high-pressure water injection pumps. On the outlet side there were gas analysis facilities and a flare and incinerator to dispose of the gas produced. It was recognised from the beginning that the relatively short period of actual gasification, and the variable quality of gas that would be produced, meant that it would not be practical to put the gas to beneficial use. Other surface facilities included a control room, electricity supply (including emergency back up), air, steam and water services.

The CRIP facility required the ability to move back the injection point. This was done with a "coiled tube" arrangement, the tubing (of about 40mm diameter) passing through a gland at the top of the injection well and with the "surplus" being coiled on a drum. The technique is widely used in the oil and gas industry, but was a first to the extent that it used stainless steel tubing (rather than the more normal carbon steel). This was necessary because the injection of pure oxygen required both special materials and special safety precautions.

Two gasification runs were carried out. The second had to be terminated due to mechanical, rather than process-related, problems.

About 300 tonnes of coal were affected during the trial, and they were either gasified or pyrolysed. The gas produced had a calorific value in the range 6-9MJ/m^3 (natural gas is about 36MJ/m^3). It contained significant amounts of nitrogen as nitrogen was injected into the outer annula of the wells for safety and cooling purposes. This should not be necessary in a commercial operation - or at least the quantities would be considerably less as a proportion of the gas produced. If the figures are calculated on a "nitrogen free" basis then the calorific value becomes about 13MJ/m^3, which is comparable to the quality obtainable from on-surface coal gasification plant .

It had been hoped to carry out a third run but this had to be abandoned due to concern, by one of the participants, that the project would run over budget. A post-burn drilling programme was subsequently undertaken to gain further information on the geometry of the cavity and the extent of gasification. It is currently intended to complete the project and vacate the site by early 1999.

The UGE trial has successfully demonstrated that:

- it is possible to drill deviated boreholes to run in, or close to, a 2m-thick coal seam located at a depth of over 500m and dipping at 30°;

- European coals can be gasified at a depth of over 500m and that good-quality gas can be produced;

- the process is stable and can be controlled;

- production can be stopped and started easily - this could be relevant for "peak-lopping" electricity generation.

In addition the trial has confirmed that:

- the ash and mineral matter associated with the coal is left underground, minimising the environmental problems of waste disposal;

- part of the sulphur content of the coal remains underground

- the sulphur in the gas is in the form of hydrogen sulphide (H_2S) and the organic nitrogen content of the coal becomes ammonia (NH_3): both of these can be removed by technology which is well established in the oil and gas industries;

- the environmental impact at the surface is lower than for conventional mining (either underground or open cast) and the potential hazards are avoided;

- the strata above the coal seam should have a low permeability;

- further work is needed on the design of the injection and ignition systems.

The way forward for the UK

The Spanish trial has shown that it is possible to gasify European coals at depth and to produce a good-quality gas. It therefore achieved its main technical objectives. The inability to run a gasifier to extinction meant that it was not possible to obtain as much economic data as originally planned. The amount of coal that can be gasified from one "set" of boreholes is critical to the overall economics.

Ideally the next stage would be to carry out a semi-commercial trial, involving a series of boreholes, and producing gas over a sufficient period of time for this to be put to beneficial use, rather than just flared. The costs of such a trial would probably require international participation and possibly also some form of EC support. It would be beneficial to carry out the trial at a UK location and consider a sequence of coal seams between 400m and 1000m deep.

So far the emphasis has been on "landward" reserves of coal, but UCG technology has wider applications. There are thick seams of high-volatile coal under the southern North Sea. These could never be mined by conventional means. The problems of access and their high spontaneous combustion risk are two reasons for this. However, they would be ideal for UCG. The costs and technical problems should not be underestimated, but it was not so many years ago that people were questioning the economics of extracting oil and gas from beneath the North Sea.

It is recognised that it is difficult for UCG to compete with current North Sea gas prices, although this could change as drilling techniques - adapted from the oil and gas industry - improve and become cheaper in real terms. However, North Sea gas is a finite resource; UCG is one option to help replace it. The timescale when it will be needed is uncertain, but there is still considerable work to be done before it can be considered a commercial system; a ten-year development period would not be unreasonable.

If a commercial UCG system could be established in the UK it would have considerable export potential for UK technology. Regions which are interested in the concept include China and India - with their increasing energy requirements - and Eastern Europe - where they want to become less dependent on natural gas from Russia.

The DTI has identified six technical and economic goals if UCG is to have any realistic opportunity of having widespread potential in the UK. These can be summarised as follows:

- Improve the accuracy of in-seam drilling to achieve a 400m run in a 2m seam, on a consistent basis. An R&D contract with one of the oil- and gas-orientated universities might be an appropriate starting point.

- Examine the implications of burning the gas produced in the Spanish UGE trial in a gas turbine. Aspects requiring consideration would be its combustion properties and possible erosion/corrosion problems.

- Produce an estimate of the landward reserves of coal which could be technically suitable for UCG. In the first instance this could be coal seams at least 2m thick and at a depth not exceeding 1200m. It has always been assumed that there were considerable reserves available that would be suitable. This needs to be validated.

- Identify a site for a semi-commercial trial of UCG. This would require a block of coal about 600m by 600m and with a seam thickness of at least 2m.

- Identify the parameters that UCG would have to meet if it were to be competitive with current North Sea oil and gas production costs.

- Carry out a pre-feasibility study for the exploitation of UCG offshore in the southern North Sea.

Next steps   The DTI and the Coal Authority will be working together to determine how best to meet the above goals over the next six years. Collaboration with other European countries may offer the most economic route to developing the technology for future commercial application now that the Spanish UCG trial has been completed. The DTI will be exploring the potential for international collaboration with the European Union and IEA countries.

Annex F

Technology Transfer and
Export Promotion Programme

Introduction

This Annex summarises the technology transfer and export promotion activities the DTI's Energy Technology Directorate plans to initiate over the next few years in collaboration with industry and the DTI's own Export Promotion Directorates.

Technology transfer

Technology transfer can be defined as the successful advancement of a technology through the technology development chain from research to commercial application in the home or overseas market. Ultimately the measure of success of any development is its commercial uptake. All technology development needs to have some market awareness, and the market drivers strengthen the closer one gets to the commercial application stage. For this reason, in shaping Government policy for cleaner coal technology, full account has been taken of the requirement to consider appropriate technology transfer mechanisms at the very beginning of this cycle - the R&D stage. This is particularly important in the main future markets of developing countries - notably China and India, together with Central and Eastern Europe, where involving their researchers and technology experts in the R&D stage of technology development should enable them to contribute to future procurement decisions based on a sound understanding of the status of technologies developed in the UK. The development of long-term relationships through R&D collaboration is seen as an important focus for the programme over the next few years to prepare the ground for future export promotion activities.

Although the label "cleaner coal technologies" is generally used to describe power generation technologies, it can be applied to any aspect of using coal or indeed some other hydrocarbons. Cleaner coal technologies can be used in the preparation and beneficiation of coal, in industrial boilers, in the steel industry and in the domestic solid fuel sector. Whilst the largest single market for cleaner coal technologies will remain the power sector, there are considerable opportunities for the export of UK components and know-how in the other sectors. Future technology transfer and export promotion activities will therefore take these markets into account.

A view of air pollution at an industrial complex near Taiyuan, Shanxi Province, China

The technology transfer and export promotion activities associated with the programme are designed to ensure that:

- the results of the programme and successful completed R&D associated with past programmes are taken up by industry as soon as possible;

- the results can be widely disseminated to support the Government's wider environmental policies, particularly to assist developing countries utilise cleaner coal technologies;

- the market barriers to technology deployment can be reduced;

- a framework is provided for UK industry and universities to develop and promote their considerable expertise and know-how in a co-ordinated and focused manner to the benefit of UK plc.

Specific measures that will be introduced to contribute to the above objectives include:

- Any project contracted via the programme must consider the exploitation of its results. Each project should have an exploitation or technology transfer plan which should be maintained through the life of the project. Each project should be revisited on an annual basis following conclusion of the work to investigate the outcome of the R&D and evaluate any successes or failures.

- Publication of a Project Profile on commencement of a project and Project Summary and Technical Report on completion of the work. For projects with an expected life of more than three years, or projects that may have a strong public interest, a mid-term review report will be published.

- Publication of Technology Status and Case Study Reports which promote the best new technology and expertise available in the UK for application in the home and overseas market.

To maximise the impact of these activities, the DTI intends to make increased use of the internet to publish details of developments in the programme and its associated publications. Details of the programme can be found under "clean coal technology" on the DTI internet site at http://www.dti.gov.uk. A range of specially commissioned articles aimed at promoting UK expertise as well as the results of successfully completed work will be initiated with advice from industry.

Export promotion

Associated with the technology transfer activities outlined above, the programme will be working in partnership with the Export Directorates of the DTI to facilitate the promotion of UK cleaner coal technology components and expertise in the main market areas, particularly China, India and a number of Central and Eastern European countries. Key activities in this area over the next few years will include:

- Publication of a range of Export Directories and Capability Brochures to promote UK expertise and components.

- Hosting industry workshops and seminars on key areas of technology development with invited audiences from key market areas.

- Trade missions, exhibitions and seminars in key markets in collaboration with Infrastructure and Energy Projects (IEP) and Export Promotion (XP) Directorates. The seminars with IEP are jointly planned and run under the auspices of the Power Sector Working Group. Missions will also include study tours for key market players to operational cleaner coal technology sites in the UK.

An important aspect of the export programme activities will be to ensure the UK clean coal technology industry makes full use of the services available from the DTI'S International Technology Service (ITS). This was established to help British business identify and learn from leading organisations around the world to improve their competitiveness at home and abroad. The programme has already been successful in helping one company arrange a secondment to the World Bank under the ITS secondment scheme, to work on cleaner coal projects for the Bank. A UK industrial delegation has visited Japan under the ITS Overseas Mission Scheme to identify areas which may benefit from collaboration on technology development as part of the Foresight exercise. Further opportunities for UK companies involved in clean coal technology development to make full use of ITS have been identified.

DTI's Overseas Trade Services (OTS), as well as providing support to trade missions, operate a Hands-on Training Scheme (HOTS) for overseas decision makers. Clean coal trade missions to China have already benefited from the support provided by OTS, and HOTS may also provide a valuable mechanism to encourage senior decision makers from the key market areas of China and India to familiarise themselves with UK technology, production methods and management skills. HOTS may offer an ideal route to promote UK clean coal technology and at the same time give potential purchasers of components valuable experience in their operation. A number of opportunities to utilise HOTS to support the objectives of the programme are being explored with industry.

Market barriers   Even if R&D is successful in developing technically viable and economically attractive technologies, there are a number of barriers to technology deployment which may limit the rate at which markets can be developed. These include:

- lack of information about the status of the technologies from impartial advisers;

- limited technical know-how to both select and operate clean coal technology effectively;

- limited knowledge of suitable innovative financing mechanisms;

- lack of a suitable market framework to allow for the investment that could modernise an existing old-fashioned power sector.

There is also a limit to the resources any one country can put into reducing these barriers. Collaboration on reducing market barriers to technology deployment has been a key priority for the IEA for a number of years, particularly where new technologies offer promise of reducing the environmental impact of the forecast substantial increase in world coal use over the next decade and beyond. In collaboration with a number of IEA countries, the DTI has initiated a range of activities aimed at reducing the impact of non-technical market barriers to technology deployment. These include:

- supporting the work of IEA Coal Research - The Clean Coal Centre, based in London, which provides an impartial and objective information and assessment service on all aspects of coal-related technologies and economics;

- supporting the preparation and publication of technology status reports, market analysis reports, finance studies etc undertaken under the auspices of the IEA;

- initiating a series of IEA best practice studies with the first aimed at optimising the efficiency of existing Chinese power stations and identifying prospects for repowering projects of interest to UK industry;

- sponsoring a range of technology and finance seminars in key market areas to raise awareness and develop future business opportunities.

Market information

There is a substantial volume of information available about clean coal technology, but it is scattered in a number of disparate sources. The programme will be preparing a guide to industry, helping to source the most up-to-date and accurate market information. Much of the material is available through various commercial and non-commercial sources, including subscription-based publications and through the World Wide Web. The difficulty for many organisations is to know where to find such information. This is particularly true for small and medium-sized enterprises (SMEs) organisations that do not have access to substantial market intelligence resources. The availability of this guide which will be updated annually, will be signposted on both the ITS internet site (http://www.dti.gov.uk/mbp/its/its.htm) and through the programme newsletter and other publications and journal articles.

Additional support for UK industry

Support for UK industry, in addition to that provided by the collaborative elements of the programme and the export promotion services of OTS and the ITS, will be provided in the form of guidance to UK companies seeking to obtain funding from the European Commission's new Fifth Framework Programme. This Programme offers support for both cleaner coal technology R&D and demonstration proposals. The first call for proposals for the Fifth Framework Programme is expected early in 1999. The DTI's experience in dealing with the European Commission can help in the preparation of UK-originated funding proposals, and the objective will be to maximise the benefits of the additional funding to UK development of cleaner coal technology.

Monitoring and evaluation

Targets will be established for each activity under the technology transfer and export promotion programme and be agreed annually with the programme contractor. The evaluation plan for the programme will incorporate mechanisms to measure the effectiveness and impact of the activities in terms of influencing awareness of UK know-how and components, enhancing networks and contribution to winning export orders.

Annex G

Details of the Evaluation and Monitoring of the Programme

Evaluation

Energy Paper 63 set out the monitoring plan for the past programme which ran from 1993 to 1998. This included a mid-term evaluation (ref. 3) which was undertaken in 1996 in order to inform the direction of the remaining years of the programme and aid consideration of a future programme.

The 1996 evaluation report detailed progress in meeting the technical and administrative objectives of the programme. Annex C lists the progress achieved in meeting these targets at the completion of the programme.

The results and recommendations of the 1996 evaluation have guided the strategy set out in this new Energy Paper. A detailed evaluation plan will be drawn up for the new programme in consultation with the DTI's Energy Policy Analysis Directorate. This mid-term evaluation will take place during the third year (2001) of the six year programme. The 1996 evaluation was undertaken by an independent panel of experts, and it is envisaged the 2001 evaluation will also be undertaken by external assessors.

Annual programme review

The programme will be reviewed annually by the DTI's Advisory Committee on Cleaner Coal Technology. The results of the review will be published each year by the DTI in an annual report approved by the Advisory Committee. The report will be made available in hard copy form and on the DTI Web site. Additionally the Advisory Committee will:

- review progress in meeting the technology and administrative targets;

- review all the collaborative programmes established with BCURA, EPSRC and the IEA;

- review the targets set for the programme in the previous year, and comment on targets proposed for the next review period, and whether the original objectives of the programme are still valid or require amendment.

Each year a detailed set of measurable targets will be established for the programme, linked to meeting the objectives agreed with industry, for the activities encompassed by the programme. These targets will be published each year in the annual report, including the extent to which the previous year's targets have been met.

Annex H

Advisory Committee on Cleaner Coal Technology

The DTI attaches considerable importance to industry being actively involved in advising on both the direction of the programme, and on which projects offer best value for money to meet the technical objectives and targets of the programme. A new Advisory Committee will be established with similar terms of reference to the Advisory Committee on Coal Research (ACCR) which it replaces. The new committee will have a membership drawn from equipment manufacturers, generating companies and universities. Representation will also be sought from the coal industry and mining equipment manufacturer trade associations, since an important role of the committee will be to advise on technology transfer and export promotion issues associated with the whole of the coal cycle. This is particularly relevant in developing countries, where coal preparation is a key issue to address in considering cleaner coal technology for power applications.

Terms of reference

- To advise the DTI, within the strategic framework set by the DTI, of the technical content of programme plans, taking due note of international programmes and other relevant work.

- To advise the DTI on the technical, economic and commercial merits of cleaner coal technology proposals and priorities, and to make recommendations on the funding of individual projects.

- To review progress of all projects supported by the programme against agreed plans and undertake an evaluation of completed projects where the DTI contribution exceeds £50,000.

- To advise the DTI on the export promotion and technology transfer activities to be initiated under the programme.

To provide a forum for the continued development of the strategic, technical and commercial aspects of UK strengths in cleaner coal technology components and expertise.

References

1. Conclusions of the Review of Energy Sources for Power Generation and Government response to fourth and fifth Reports of the Trade and Industry Committee. Command 4071, DTI, October 1998.

2. Energy Paper 63 - Clean Coal Technologies: A Strategy for the Coal R&D Programme. DTI, October 1994.

3. Interim Evaluation of the Coal Research and Development Programme of the UK DTI. July 1996. Report No. Coal R086, available from Energy Technology Directorate, DTI.

4. International Energy Agency World Energy Outlook, 1998 Edition.

5. Private Communication, Federation of British Electrotechnical and Allied Manufacturers' Associations (BEAMA), 1998.

6. Our Competitive Future: Building the Knowledge-Driven Economy. The Government's Competitiveness White Paper, Command 4176, DTI, December 1998.

7. Realising our Potential: A Strategy for Science, Engineering and Technology. Command 2250, DTI, May 1993.

8. Blueprint for the next round of Foresight, DTI, December 1998.

9. Clean Coal Technology - Markets and Opportunities to 2010. IEA/DTI, 1996. Report available from Energy Technology Directorate, DTI.

10. Industry Perspectives on Cleaner Coal Technology, Torrens I. IEA Cleaner Coal Technology Workshop, Feb 1997.

11. IGCC: From the Drawing Board to Commercial Service, Chambers A. Power Engineering International, Jan/Feb 1998.

12. Power Generation Equipment Supplement, Financial Times, 19 June 1997.

13. Factors Affecting the Take-up of Clean Coal Technologies, Overview Report, Coal Industry Advisory Board, IEA, 1996.

14. Supercritical Steam Cycles for Power Generation Applications. Technology Status Report. TSR 009. DTI Cleaner Coal Technology Programme. January 1999.

15. Gasification of Solid and Liquid Fuels for Power Generation. Technology Status Report. TSR 008. DTI Cleaner Coal Technology Programme. December 1998.

16. Competitiveness of Future Coal-fired units in Different Countries, Scott D and Nilsson P-A. Report no. CCC/14. Published by IEA Coal Research - The Clean Coal Centre, ISBN 92-9029-320-9, Jan 1999.

17. Coal Bed Methane Extraction, Davidson R, Sloss L and Clarke L. Report no. IEACR/76. Published by IEA Coal Research - The Clean Coal Centre, ISBN 92-9029-248-2, Jan 1995.

Glossary

British Coal Utilisation Research Association (BCURA): Originally established in 1938, BCURA became a registered charity in 1976. The aim of BCURA is to promote research and other activities concerned with the production, distribution and use of coal and its derivatives. As part of this aim BCURA offers grants to academic institutions to undertake research in the field of coal science. These grants have typically supported postgraduate or post-doctoral research and have taken the form of a bursary in addition to allowing for the purchase of research equipment.

Carbon dioxide (CO_2): CO_2 is produced when fuels containing carbon are burned. CO_2 contributes about 60% of the global warming effect of man-made greenhouse gas emissions CO_2 is emitted naturally by living organisms, but these emissions are balanced by the absorption of CO_2 by plant during photosynthesis (the manufacture of carbohydrates for growth). Burning of fossil fuels, however, releases carbon fixed by plant millions of years ago, at a rate much faster than plant now can absorb it, thereby increasing the concentration of CO_2 in the atmosphere.

Carbon intensity: Fuels differ in the amount of carbon they contain. Coal has much more than natural gas (which has more hydrogen), so burning coal will inevitably produce more emitted carbon than an equivalent amount of gas. Allowing also for the greater conversion efficiency of combined cycle gas turbine electricity stations, a unit of electricity generated from coal will produce more than twice as much carbon dioxide as a unit produced from gas.

Carbon sequestration: This is a general term for processes which remove carbon dioxide from the atmosphere. Natural sequestration occurs mainly through the use of carbon dioxide by growing green plant (photosynthesis), and increased forest planting has been suggested as a means of absorbing, at least temporarily, some of the extra emissions arising from human activity. It is also technically feasible, though costly, to capture directly the carbon dioxide from large, man-made sources such as fossil-fuel burning power stations, and then store it away from the atmosphere in depleted natural oil or gas wells, or in deep aquifers. (For an example, see website http://www.ieagreen.org.uk).

Cleaner coal technologies: Technologies designed to enhance both the conversion efficiency and the environmental acceptability of coal extraction, preparation and use. The term is usually used to describe advanced coal power generation technologies which have efficiencies of 42% or more (on lower heating value (LHV) basis), with low emissions of sulphur and nitrogen oxides.

Coal Authority: The Coal Authority, which was established by the Coal Industry Act 1994, is a Non-Departmental Public Body sponsored by the DTI. Its chief duties are: to license and lease coal-mining operations, with a view to securing an economically viable industry; to manage certain liabilities associated with former coal-mining; and to provide information on coal-mining matters.

Coal Research Forum: The Coal Research Forum was established by industry and the academic community in 1988 to encourage, promote and co-ordinate basic research on coal, coal products and coal utilisation in the UK, with particular emphasis on:

- promotion and co-ordination of contact between academe and industry;

- the assessment and co-ordination of resources and needs concerned with coal utilisation and conversion.

Efficiency (overall power plant efficiency): The efficiency with which heat energy contained in fuel is converted into electrical energy. Efficiencies quoted in this document (including the Annexes) are based on the lower heating value (LHV) of the fuel which, according to the following formula:

$$\text{Efficiency} = \frac{\text{Amount of net electricity generated}}{\text{Heat input from the fuel}}$$

gives a higher value than is generally achieved in practice. Efficiency based on net calorific value (or LHV) is higher than the efficiency based on a gross calorific value (higher heating value - HHV). The difference between LHV and HHV (which can also be used to define the efficiency of plant) is due to the energy associated with the latent heat of evaporation of water products from the steam cycle which cannot be recovered and put to economic use.

Temperature of cooling water is a significant factor in efficiencies achievable in practice. Generally, the lower the temperature of cooling water, the higher the efficiencies obtained. This factor should be borne in mind when comparing efficiencies between countries. Energy used in emission abatement equipment, such as FGD, will also clearly affect the overall efficiency of the plant. The efficiencies quoted in this Paper assume FGD plant has been fitted for both subcritical and supercritical plant, with the exception for the average efficiency of plant in developing countries such as China.

Engineering and Physical Sciences Research Council: EPSRC acts on behalf of Government in supporting research and postgraduate training in engineering and physical sciences. Its mission is "to promote and support high quality basic, strategic and applied research and related postgraduate training in engineering and the physical sciences, placing special emphasis on meeting the needs of users of its research and training outputs, thereby enhancing the UK's competitiveness and quality of life". Further information about EPSRC can be found via the internet: http:\\www.epsrc.ac.uk

Flue gas desulphurisation (FGD): FGD is a process for removing sulphur dioxide (SO_2 - a contributor to acid rain and smog) from the flue gases of power stations after combustion. There are a number of possible technologies for doing this: the ones used in the UK are the wet lime or limestone-gypsum processes. These consume limestone and water and produce gypsum (calcium sulphate) and CO_2. FGD can remove (under ideal circumstances) 90-95% of the SO_2 in flue gases and can also help absorb dust or particulates. Fitment of FGD slightly reduces the conversion efficiency of the generation process because of the power needed to run the unit.

Foresight: The Technology Foresight exercise was initiated by the UK Government in 1994. It brought together industrialists from specific industrial sectors and academics to identify the market and technical opportunities that are likely to emerge over the next 20 years. Sector-specific panels identified those opportunities that impact on wealth creation and/or the quality of life and recommended the investments and actions required to implement them. Considerable emphasis is placed on networking to ensure that business people, engineers and scientists are better informed about each other's efforts.

Greenhouse effect and climate change: A natural greenhouse effect raises the temperature of the Earth's surface by 33°C, on average, thus making possible most plant and animal life as we know it. About one third of the sunlight reaching the Earth is reflected back into space. The other two thirds is absorbed at the Earth's surface, warming it up, and from which it is re-radiated as invisible, infra-red (or heat) radiation. Some of this is in turn absorbed by certain gases in the atmosphere, thereby making it warmer near the surface, in the same way that the glass in a greenhouse traps heat on the inside. Naturally occurring "greenhouse gases" include water vapour, carbon dioxide (CO_2), methane (CH_4) and nitrous oxide (N_2O).

Any factor which alters the amount of radiation received from the Sun or lost to space may influence the climate by changing the temperatures at the Earth's surface and in the atmosphere. Thus any change in the greenhouse effect is a cause for concern. Human activity is known to be emitting extra amounts of greenhouse gases, which will tend to alter the amounts of radiated energy trapped by the atmosphere, and so may have an effect on climate.

International Energy Agency (IEA): The IEA is an autonomous body which was established in November 1974 within the framework of the Organisation for Economic Co-operation and Development (OECD) to implement an international energy programme. It carries out a comprehensive programme of energy co-operation among 24 of the OECD's 29 member countries. The basic aims of the IEA are:

i) co-operation among IEA participating countries to reduce excessive dependence on oil through energy conservation; development of alternative energy sources and energy R&D;

ii) an information system on the international oil market as well as consultation with oil companies;

iii) co-operation with oil-producing and other oil-consuming countries with a view to developing a stable international energy trade as well as the rational management and use of world energy resources in the interest of all countries;

iv) a plan to prepare participating countries against the risk of a major disruption of oil supplies and to share available oil in the event of an emergency.

IEA participating countries are Australia, Austria, Belgium, Canada, Denmark, Finland, France, Germany, Greece, Hungary, Ireland, Italy, Japan, Luxembourg, the Netherlands, New Zealand, Norway, Portugal, Spain, Sweden, Switzerland, Turkey, the United Kingdom, the United States. The Commission of the European Communities takes part in the work of the IEA.

Low-NO$_X$ burners: Low-NO$_X$ burners can be installed on either new or existing combustion plant. By controlling the initial mixing of air and fuel, they maintain temperature and oxygen levels in critical parts of the flame at the minimum level necessary for effective combustion. This greatly reduces the opportunities for NO$_X$ production. Low-NO$_X$ burners can generally reduce NO$_X$ concentrations by 30-60% (up to 70% with some latest designs of burners).

Organisation for Economic Co-operation and Development (OECD): The OECD was established in 1960 and promotes policies designed:

- to achieve the highest sustainable economic growth and employment and a rising standard of living in Member countries, while maintaining financial stability, and thus to contribute to the development of the world economy;

- to contribute to sound economic expansion in Member as well as non-member countries in the process of economic development;

- to contribute to the expansion of world trade on a multilateral, non-discriminatory basis in accordance with international obligations.

Power Sector Working Group: In 1993 Richard Needham, then Minister for Trade at the DTI, announced the establishment of a number of Sector Working Groups with the specific remit of considering ways in which the project export performance of UK plc could be enhanced.

Five working groups - covering power, airports, water, railways and ports - are now in existence, operating as partnerships between the DTI's Infrastructure and Energy Projects Directorate (IEP), which provides the secretariat to each group, and the private sector, which provides a chairman for each group and the majority of the members.

The Power Sector Working Group is currently under the chairmanship of David Jefferies, Chairman of the National Grid Company plc, with a membership drawn from the most influential companies in the UK power sector and from all sections of the industry, ie consultant engineers, generators, operator/investors and distribution companies; it also includes specialist service providers, such as bankers and lawyers, with the industry trade association, BEAMA (Federation of British Electrotechnical and Allied Manufacturers' Associations), there to ensure that news of the group's work is disseminated across the entire electricity supply industry.

Reburn technology: Substantial reductions in NO$_X$ emissions can be achieved by burning up to around 20% of natural gas or coal, as reburn fuel, at the top of a coal-fired boiler. The reburn fuel reacts with the NO$_X$ created by the burning of coal below to produce nitrogen.

ROAME Statement: Any DTI programme involving a significant level of resources, eg over £1 million, must have an agreed ROAME Statement before expenditure can be incurred. ROAME is a statement setting out what the proposed activity is, the justification for such Government action (Rationale), the objectives of the activity (Objectives), how individual projects within the programme will be selected (Appraisal), how the progress of the activity will be monitored (Monitoring) and how the effectiveness of the programme will be evaluated (Evaluation).

Small and medium-sized enterprises (SMEs): For the purpose of this paper, SMEs are defined as companies with workforces of less than 250 employees.

Stoker-fired boilers: There are a number of stoker-fired boiler designs but these are no longer used in the UK for large-scale generation of electricity, having been superseded by more efficient pulverised fuel boilers. The most familiar at larger scale is the chain grate and related travelling grate. The grate consists of a driven looped mat of metallic links, the top surface of which receives coal from a hopper at the front end of the boiler. Primary combustion air is provided through the coal bed from below and coal ignition effected by radiation from a refractory arch above the bed. Burnout takes place along the grate and ash is removed at the far end.

Printed in the United Kingdom for The Stationery Office
J77593, C8, 4/99, 5673.